Battle Rock

Battle Rock

The Struggle Over a One-Room School

in America's Vanishing West

William Celis

BSB

PublicAffairs

New York

Published in the United States by PublicAffairs™,
a member of the Perseus Books Group.
All rights reserved.
Printed in the United States of America.

No part of this book may be reproduced in any manner whatsoever without written
permission except in the case of brief quotations embodied in critical articles and
reviews. For information, address PublicAffairs, 250 West 57th Street, Suite 1321,
New York, NY 10107. PublicAffairs books are available at special discounts for bulk
purchases in the U.S. by corporations, institutions, and other organizations. For
more information, please contact the Special Markets Department at The Perseus
Books Group, 11 Cambridge Center, Cambridge, MA 02142, or call (617) 252-5298.

Book design by Jane Raese.

Library of Congress Cataloging-in-Publication Data
Battle Rock: the struggle over a one-room school in America's vanishing West /
William Celis.
p. cm.
ISBN 1-891620-66-5
1. Battle Rock Charter School (Montezuma County, Colo.)
2. Rural schools—Colorado—Cortez.
I. Title.
LD7501.C87613 C45 2002
372.9788'27—DC21
2002031829

FIRST EDITION

1 3 5 7 9 10 8 6 4 2

For my parents,
William and Aurora Celis,

and my friend,
Willis Charles Jackson
(1945–2001)

Contents

Acknowledgments

My thanks to McElmo Canyon residents whose candor made this book possible and, in particular, Stephen Hanson and the children who attended Battle Rock during the 1999–2000 school year.

Stephen and his wife, Susan, along with Audrey Allmon, Bill and Teresa Blakney, Ed and Alice Baltes, John and Brenda Burns, Roger Hazlewood, Chris and Andrea Jeter, Eric and Kim Lindgren, Paul and Tumiko Murphy, and Sheldon and Naomi Zwicker, repeatedly opened their homes and lives to me. Their honesty made this a richer book.

Suzy Meyer, the general manager and editor of the *Cortez Journal,* regularly during the year fielded my questions about the local culture. David Staats, the managing editor of the *Durango Herald* and a grad school classmate, provided additional insight into the Four Corners region of the United States, as well as his good company. The staff of the Cortez Public Library helped me go through decades of vintage newspapers and track down information, as did local author Fred Blackburn. My thanks, too, to the Reverend Don Henderson and the congregation of the First Assembly of God. Many other Montezuma County residents, public officials and private citizens, rural and urban, were exceedingly open and supportive of my efforts during my year in Cortez.

Sam Roberts, the deputy editor of the *New York Times*'s "Week in Review," commissioned the June 1996 article that became the genesis of this book, and Sam later read early drafts of a proposal that ultimately became this book. Patricia Nelson Limerick, one of the country's leading historians about the West and a professor at the University of Colorado at Boulder, also offered insights, and lifelines, during the proposal writing process.

Matt Bialer, my agent at Trident Media, took what I sent him and pushed and prodded me through additional drafts, producing a proposal that ultimately succeeded. As chapters began taking form, several friends and colleagues read drafts and offered frank feedback. Thanks to Tim Burgess, Roz Dauber, Charlotte Laughlin, Lauraine Miller, Sam Roberts, Cynthia Sanz, Ronnie Joe Smith, Judy Twersky, and Lena Williams. Other friends and University of Southern California colleagues, Laura Castañeda, Cheryl Devall, Neal Koch, Debra Ono, James Vasquez, Luis Delgado, Omar Vega, and Jesus Olivares, offered words of support when I needed them.

At the Education Commission of the States in Denver, I am indebted to Chris Pipho and Kathy Christie for their assistance and their willingness to let me browse ECS's impressive library. At the U.S. Department of Education, my thanks go to Vance Grant, who dug through statistics of every sort with good cheer and amazing efficiency. The U.S. Department of Agriculture and its Economic Forecast Service provided the most penetrating data on cultural and economic life in rural America. And the people at the Annenberg Rural Challenge and its later incarnation, the Rural School and Community Trust, provided me with reports about the progress of schools across the country like Battle Rock.

My editor at PublicAffairs, Robert Kimzey, possesses a rare blend of humor, patience, and wisdom. His love for the written word and his encouragement helped sustain me through several revisions. My thanks to him and to Peter Osnos, the publisher of PublicAffairs, for their support of this project and the attention they gave it. I also thank copy editor Steven Baker for a careful and thorough reading that improved the manuscript immeasurably.

In addition to a generous advance from PublicAffairs, my early work on this book was funded by the Freedom Forum Professors' Publishing Program. I thank Félix Gutiérrez, a former senior vice president of the Freedom Forum's Pacific Coast Center in San Francisco and now a colleague at USC.

Most of this book was written and revised while I was a journalism professor at the USC Annenberg School for Communication. I received a reduced teaching load to help me complete the manuscript, and my thanks go to Dean Geoffrey Cowan and Michael Parks, current director of the journalism school, for their unwavering support. I also thank Loren Ghiglione, then the director of the Annenberg journalism school and now the dean of the Medill School of Journalism at Northwestern University, who granted me the reduced teaching load during my first year at USC.

Finally, this book is dedicated to my parents, William and Aurora Lozano Celis of San Antonio, who taught me the importance of a strong work ethic. They grew up in an era when Mexican-Americans rarely finished public school and fewer still went to college. Their generation opened doors so that I could take advantage of opportunities they didn't have. My sisters, Annette Garcia, Liz Loftis, and Laura M. Celis, and my aunt, Yolanda Hernandez, provided long-distance support.

The same could be said of my good friend and mentor Willis Charles Jackson, former editor of the *Oakland Tribune,* who passed away during the writing of this book after a long illness. Chuck was an editor ahead of his time. As an African-American, he preached the virtue of diversity long before it was in vogue. He launched the careers of dozens of journalists of color, many of whom now work at the nation's leading dailies and broadcast networks. I had the good fortune of working for Chuck twenty years ago when he returned to his native Fort Worth after several years at the *Washington Post.* And over the years, Chuck and his wife, Deidra "June" Keels Jackson, became touchstones and, in short, a second family.

Foreword

*D*eep *in the rural southwest corner of Colorado,* in the Four Corners region, the residents of McElmo Canyon embraced tradition as strongly as they rebuffed change. For most of the twentieth century, some canyon residents lived entire lives in dwellings without indoor plumbing. Others resided in homes warmed only by wood-burning stoves. Life and death occurred on the same patch of land. The dead were buried in handmade coffins and interred in family plots, not far from the farmhouses in which they were born. So tightly bound was the picture postcard community that for eighty years most of the children enrolled in the canyon's one-room school were related.

But in the 1990s, as McElmo Canyon neared the end of one century and the beginning of another, the community began a rapid, if reluctant, makeover. The isolation was stripped away as urban families moved to the canyon in greater numbers. They erected homes that were, by local standards, large and ostentatious. Telephone party lines disappeared. The old gravel road that snaked along the canyon floor was finally paved, and most of the children attending the one-room school were no longer related.

As McElmo Canyon went, so went much of rural America. By the end of the 1990s, urban people had moved to rural communities in numbers so great the decade produced one of rural America's biggest population booms of the twentieth century, second only to the 1970s. During the 1990s, rural America grew by 5.2 million people; nearly three-fourths of that growth was the result of migration. In the 1980s, by comparison, rural counties grew by only 1.3 million, much of the gain the result of births, according to demographers at Loyola University and the U.S. Department of Agriculture. In all, nearly 74 percent of the nation's 2,303 rural counties grew in the 1990s as compared with just 45 percent in the 1980s. No matter how the numbers were parsed, the statistics produced a snapshot so startling that rural Americans rubbed their eyes in collective disbelief. Who were these new neighbors?

They were young families, single college-aged people, mature single adults, whites and people of color, straights and gays and lesbians, arriving from Chicago, Los Angeles, Seattle, Houston, and other major cities. Representing every rung of the economic ladder, these new pioneers settled in small towns in New England, the Deep South, the Plains, the Pacific Northwest, and McElmo Canyon and other rustic communities in the West, which recorded the steepest population gains of any region. Some were returning to their rural roots; others wanted safe schools for their children. More yearned for the tranquility of a small town.

I was among the urban wave moving to rural America, but for reasons entirely different than most of my fellow urban expatriates. I was intrigued by rural America's renaissance. The story initially piqued my interest when I wrote about McElmo Canyon's one-room charter school in 1996 for the *New York Times,* where I had been an education correspondent before leaving to teach at the University of Colorado. Many of the one-room schools, I reported, were reopened or reconstituted as charter schools, a form of public school that gives parents more control over their children's education. During the next two years, I thought often of McElmo Canyon and its school. There was something about a rural school nearly one hundred years old sitting in a canyon larger than the island of Manhattan that stirred the imagination. So in 1999 I took a leave from my teaching job and moved to Cortez, the nearest town to McElmo Canyon, and the seat of Montezuma County. I dedicated the next year to exploring a story that had most of my friends wondering whether I had lost my mind.

"You're doing what?" a New York friend asked me when I told her where I was moving. "Are you crazy?"

Perhaps, I said. But after four fairly sedate years in Boulder, I was keen on exploring a place as foreign to my New York friends as New York is to most of the people I write about in this book. I also had a personal reason for my journey. I had fond memories of working on rural newspapers as a young journalist in my native Texas. As I explored my new community, stripping away layer upon layer, I found a rich story that most of the national media missed: the radical makeover of the American countryside. Besides their sheer numbers, urban people helped breathe new life into failing rural institutions, including the nearly extinct one-room school.

For the first time in seven decades, the number of one-room schools increased in the 1993–1994 school year, according to a survey by the U.S. Department of Education, which defines one-room schools in its survey as "one-teacher" schools. More often than not, these one-teacher schools were one room, perhaps two rooms, and their growth was no aberration. Thirty-five one-room schools were reopened from 1993 to 1998, a five-year period that produced the only sustained growth of one-room schools in the twentieth century. By the end of 1998, 476 one-teacher schools were in operation, up from 441 five years before.

What some demographers called the rural rebound included the countryside's tattered infrastructure. Roads and bridges were built or improved, and high-powered telephone lines were installed to accommodate rising Internet use. Corporations and foundations gave millions of dollars to rural campaigns of every stripe, from education to the arts to economic development, which remained the last and most challenging hurdle to rural America's full recovery.

The rural economy, though posting solid gains in the early 1990s, remained uneven, the result of thin or undereducated workforces. Many communities still languished from the ruinous collapse of the farm economy a decade earlier. Others were simply too remote or too far gone from years of a slow bleed to enjoy the boom. But many communities reaped the benefits of this revival.

There was, however, a predictable downside. As more city people called rural America home, real estate prices escalated, communities experienced their first traffic jams, prices increased for consumer goods, and not surprisingly, rural people and their new urban neighbors clashed. McElmo Canyon's topography contributed to an "us against them" mentality. Longtime canyon residents who had tilled or ranched the rich canyon floor for generations lived in the western half, their landholdings amounting to thousands of acres. The canyon's eastern end was inhabited by urban families who had purchased smaller home sites created by the repeated parceling of land sold by farmers and ranchers. As west-canyon residents peered at their new neighbors to the east and the gaze was returned, McElmo Canyon's much-beloved one-room school sat in the middle, on a sort of Mason-Dixon line. At times, the Battle Rock school seemed aptly named.

The mix of rural and urban sensibilities proved so toxic that teachers were fired, then rehired. Some teachers were permanently run out of the canyon. The one-room school had long provided the glue that bound the community's heart and soul. But now with the adhesive gone, or at least stretched thin by all the fighting, rural life was hardly the bucolic existence that urban people had anticipated or that rural people had long embraced.

"One must walk very quietly here if you're from a city," one urban expatriate living in McElmo Canyon warned me. "It's like a civil war."

M*y education as a rural American* began quickly. I naively came to my new home embracing the notion that small communities were simple and friendly. I soon discovered that these small-town qualities were myths perpetrated by Norman Rockwell's paintings, the enduring image of Main Street, and popular television shows featuring fictionalized towns like Mayberry. Small towns were simpler places to live than cities, of course, but only in the strictest sense. Driving from my house to the grocery store wasn't typically a bumper-to-bumper traffic experience. Rural America, I discovered in my early weeks in Cortez, was just as complicated as cities but in wholly different ways. Most urban expatriates moving to Montezuma County were unaware of this, including me. All of us learned, some painfully.

To locals, I was the man from New York writing about them. Never mind that I was from Texas. I stopped correcting people after realizing it didn't matter whether I was a New Yorker, a Texan, or a Martian. I was another outsider moving to Montezuma County to upset a way of life that was quickly vanishing. There weren't many welcome mats in my first weeks.

People shunned me. They canceled scheduled interviews. They avoided me when I saw them at the grocery store, the post office, or the local Wal-Mart. As a Mexican-American, I encountered racism. I saw poverty that rivaled what I had seen in Appalachia as a journalist. Rural stubbornness to change was astounding and disturbing. So were the blind spots of some urban expatriates. I heard them condescend to sales clerks and loudly deride their new home. I likened them to people who tracked mud into the house with no apologies.

But when I peeled away the layers of Cortez's off-putting and crusty exterior, there were elements of Norman Rockwell's

America. A person's word still carried weight. Personal responsibility was still a virtue in ample supply. Most people still attended church regularly, and they tithed their 10 percent. Neighbors still helped one another to an extent I did not see in cities. Invitations soon came from urban families, but those were followed by ones from rural people.

Here was a place where the richness of life was there for the picking, literally and figuratively. I strained my back harvesting apples and plucked wild plums with schoolboys. I attended rural churches and experienced old-time religion. I watched my Thanksgiving turkey killed by three rifle shots. I helped herd cattle during a spring drive when temperatures hit a hundred degrees or more. I received fresh vegetables and fruit, homemade bread and pies, and jellies and jams.

In reading about McElmo Canyon and its school, about the people of Cortez and Montezuma County, people will be reading about themselves, their dreams, their aspirations. For in all of us, there is a bit of a small town, the need to connect, to breathe, and to simply live.

Battle Rock

Part I

Chapter 1

Battle Rock

*B*efore the first hint of day spilled over the rugged rim of McElmo Canyon, Stephen Hanson's white Ford Explorer rolled into the gravel parking lot of the school. There was hardly a sound at that hour of the morning, much of the world still asleep. The silence was broken only by the wind blowing through a stand of cottonwood trees guarding the school, or by an occasional passing car or truck. Their headlights pierced the darkness, and for an instant, a rustic wood sign appeared next to the meandering canyon road:

BATTLE ROCK . . .
A COMMUNITY SCHOOL SITE
SINCE 1915.

The one-room school sat in the heart of a twenty-five-mile-long canyon, and its red, white, and pink eighteen-inch-thick sandstone walls matched the colors of the canyon's imposing corridor. The building's narrow, rectangular windows looked out like sharp-eyed sentries over a playground holding a swing set, a basketball court, and a jungle gym. Beyond the playground stood a small white-frame dwelling that once housed the school's teachers. The simply constructed teacherage, as it was once called, now housed music and art lessons.

Stephen worked quickly in the tiny classroom, where the smell of freshly waxed hardwood floors penetrated the air. He set up two filing cabinets and installed a water filter on the school's tap, the water drawn from a two-hundred-foot-deep well behind the school. Virtually every wall had bookshelves. A large map of Native American tribal lands on another wall reminded students they shared this great expanse of country with the Navajo, the Hopi, and the Ute Mountain Ute. On the chalkboard, its clean sheen ready for the year's academic assault, Stephen wrote with textbook precision: August 30, 1999.

Paul Stephen Hanson looked younger than his forty-eight years. His light-brown eyes were complemented by a brown mustache flecked with traces of gray, and his long brown hair reached to the middle of his back, clipped neatly into a ponytail by an antique silver button. Dressed this morning in jeans and a lightweight blue shirt, he sometimes came to school in shorts when the weather turned hot. His voice resonated, one of the many tools in his teaching arsenal that kept his students focused. At six feet and with a rugged build, he cut an imposing figure in the classroom, but he wasn't so formidable that students didn't feel comfortable hugging him on occasion.

Stephen was beginning his sixth year at the tiny school, and he had often thought about pursuing another line of work. But when the bus driver one early fall day that year asked if he was ready for another school year, the teacher smiled, and his brown eyes twinkled.

"What else would I do?" he asked.

Stephen wasn't being flippant, for he had tried his hand at several vocations. For the last twenty years, he had pursued seemingly disparate careers in the United States and Australia, bouncing between the two continents like a diplomat. When he graduated from Pacific Lutheran College, he went halfway around the world to teach in a school for aboriginal students on an island in Australia's Great Barrier Reef. But he chafed under the paternalistic ways white Australians treated the native people. One day he quit, just flat walked out of a faculty meeting at the school in a fit of anger over the backward ways in which the school educated its students. He began growing his trademark ponytail, a thumb in the face to his Australian administrators, who wore their hair in short-cropped conservative cuts and who had created what Stephen considered rigid, sometimes punishing bureaucracies. He found work at a nearby Catholic elementary school, where he drew the disfavor of the white priests by dating a woman named Elizabeth, Australia's first aboriginal supermodel. He married her and traveled in her circles, rubbing elbows with Australian tennis champion Evonne Goolagong and pop star Olivia Newton-John.

He also became a newspaper reporter, editor, and publisher of two Australian newspapers that served the country's native population. The first, funded by the government, was shut down when it began criticizing what Stephen felt were punitive policies that kept the aboriginal population in its place. The second paper, the *Palm Island Voice,* the more successful of the two, served a population of largely undereducated aborigines; hence, it carried a lot of color pictures and, like the first paper for which Stephen had worked, managed to write articles about white Australian racism. The paper folded, but not from government censorship. Its circulation of three hundred did not support monthly costs of $5,000.

"It was the most fun I ever had on a job," he told me during one of our dinners. "I flew in a little prop plane for hundreds of miles to the bush, reported a story, and took some pictures and then had drinks in a bar."

In between his Australian jobs, he came to the Four Corners

region, where his parents had retired, and ultimately became the principal of a Navajo school in New Mexico. But Australia always seemed to beckon, and Stephen returned a final time to try his hand at oyster and giant clam farming. That effort also went bust. But before Stephen left Australia, he and a friend visiting from McElmo Canyon motored out to the reef, dived in, and harvested as many oysters and clams as they could eat. When the party was over, the Hanson family moved to Cortez for the last and final time, where Stephen became a carpenter and home builder and then opened a butcher and meat-processing business with his father and a brother. Along the way, Stephen's twenty-year marriage collapsed. Elizabeth returned to Australia, and Stephen kept their two sons.

His careers came together like pieces of a puzzle in the classroom, where his experiences gave him the tools to be a good teacher. Living with people of color on two continents and teaching in schools for Native Americans and aboriginal children, he also acquired sensibilities uncommon for most white men. He knew more about minority groups than many of his white friends, and it bothered him that the name of the county in which McElmo Canyon sat was spelled *Montezuma* instead of *Moctezuma,* the correct spelling of the Aztec ruler's name. He encouraged his students to read about the Holocaust, the Civil Rights Movement, and black women in particular because, the teacher once said, he "found black women in American history incredible people, given all their accomplishments and what they had to go through to achieve what they did."

*S*tephen and I had met a year earlier when, on a hunch, I packed my Jeep and made the eight-hour drive through the Rocky Mountains from Boulder to Cortez. The school had been included in a story I had written for the *New York Times* about the mid-1990s comeback of the rural school. I intuitively knew there was more to this school than two paragraphs in an eight-hundred-word "Week in Review" story. Stephen was accustomed to a variety of visitors at Battle Rock, and he greeted me with an easy style. After spending a day with him and the children, I knew I wanted to return. Fourteen months later, I did.

A week before classes began, Stephen introduced me to the school board, and as I left that night, he smiled and said, "I guess we'll be seeing a lot of each other."

When Stephen arrived that first day of school, I was already there. I woke up early that morning, stopped at the Texaco Amigo Mart in downtown Cortez to buy a brown bag lunch and then, driving through the empty streets of the shuttered town, started the thirty-mile trip to Battle Rock. I helped him unload his Explorer and then stood back and watched him work hurriedly on paperwork. In about an hour, Stephen's twenty-six students in kindergarten through the sixth grade were scheduled to take their places at the half-dozen tables that served as their desks.

Because I had already visited the school a year earlier, I knew what to expect that first day. The children pursued different lessons at different times of the day. The teacher launched the younger students on reading or grammar lessons. While the younger children were working on their assignments, he tested older students on reading comprehension. Stephen answered the phone, responded to email, and greeted visiting parents. He opened and sorted the school's mail. He served as the school's accountant, paying Battle Rock's bills. At the end of the day, he sometimes even helped the janitor clean the school.

Stephen made teaching in a multigrade classroom look deceptively easy, but he had help. Battle Rock boasted several part-time teachers who taught math and science, Spanish, music, and art. When they weren't at the school and when Stephen was on the telephone or working intensely with one student, the older kids helped their younger classmates—the theory being that children had a language all their own and no adult could speak it. But someone had to orchestrate this symphony of learning, which sometimes looked and sounded chaotic, and Battle Rock's conductor was Stephen Hanson.

When he took over Battle Rock in 1993, the school was country, heart and soul, but it had traveled miles in its sensibilities. Gone were the days when children arrived shoeless and on horseback. Central heat had long replaced the potbellied stove that had squatted for decades in the middle of the room, though the burn marks from its three legs were still discernable on the hardwood floor. No longer did the teacher make lunch in a large cauldron in the schoolroom with whatever the parents had sent to school that day—beans, potatoes, or perhaps a bit of chicken, venison, or elk. These days, microwave ovens warmed the lunches the children brought from home. The school had long surrendered the military-like line of wooden desks in favor of round tables. Sitting along one wall were five computers stuffed with educational software that transported students far beyond McElmo Canyon. The school's emphasis on outdoor education was perhaps the only vestige of another time.

Stephen used the surrounding canyon for geology lessons and the dimensions of the ancient Battle Rock Cemetery to formulate and calculate math equations. Wildlife, dead or alive, offered opportunities for study. One year, the children dissected a flattened fox found on McElmo Canyon Road. The bushy hide still hung from a tree near the old teacherage. Stephen led hikes up the canyon wall, to waterfalls and deep shimmering pools and to the well-preserved ruins of the Anasazi, ancient people who inhabited the Four Corners region a millennium ago.

Battle Rock was not a typical one-room school, but neither was Stephen Hanson an average one-room schoolteacher. As the sun's first rays spilled through the narrow windows and fell across the shiny hardwood floor, he looked at a wall clock, its hands approaching 7 A.M.

"If you want to catch the bus with the kids, you better leave now," he told me. I hurried to my Jeep and drove back to town to catch the bus. The canyon was bathed in warm sunlight.

A half-dozen cars and trucks sat along a chain-link fence near a Mobil Corporation field office at the western edge of nearby Cortez as children and their parents waited for the Battle Rock bus. Bus no. 9 turned on McElmo Canyon Road from town, sputtering as it pulled into the parking lot. I boarded the bus and waited for the children.

Kayla, a sixth grader entering her final year at the school, climbed the bus's black rubber steps, followed by eight other students. The rosy-cheeked girl smiled at Debbie, who had driven eighteen-wheel rigs for a living before driving buses for the Montezuma-Cortez School District.

"Hi, nice to see you again!" said Debbie, whose face was framed by wavy red hair. She greeted each of her young passengers above the cacophony of the bus's motor. "Did you have a good summer?"

Shane, Kayla's younger brother, followed at his sister's heels, and one by one the remaining students climbed aboard. The students were all "townies" whose parents could have sent their children to schools in town. Instead they chose a one-room school some twenty miles deep into the heart of the canyon because of its special blend of education.

The bus began its descent into McElmo Canyon, past the bobbing sunflowers, the boulders and cedar and juniper trees, and past a weathered sign that read WINDING ROAD NEXT 25 MILES. The road veered sharply around a large boulder that leaned over the road and towered over the bus. Beyond the boulder lay an expansive canyon with deep gorges, soaring walls, and spectacular outcroppings in hues of pink, red, and white. The children had seen the canyon so many times before that they were indifferent to the spectacular sight that unfolded before them. I had driven down the canyon a handful of times to meet with Stephen, but this marked the first time someone else was doing the driving, and that allowed me to take in my extraordinary new home.

The surrounding terrain kept McElmo Canyon a well-guarded secret, for there was no indication that a yawning canyon sat at the western edge of Cortez—with over 8,000 residents, the closest town with amenities. The late-summer wildflowers, gray-hued sage, and rabbit brush, topped with yellow blossoms, grew so thickly that sometimes the luxurious growth spilled onto the edges of the twisting road, a welcome mat for the children of Battle Rock.

The canyon was largely untamed land, the rolling terrain giving way to the sheer canyon walls that soared, at their highest points, some 1,000 feet or more above the canyon floor. Every few miles, the swells gave way to level land. It was here, where the land relaxed, that the earth was tilled for crops and gardens that sat next to the newer vineyards planted by urban residents. Cows, horses, sheep, and goats grazed, alongside the ostriches and llamas that urban transplants had introduced to the canyon's livestock. Restored century-old stone houses made of the canyon's colorful Dakota sandstone dotted the landscape. So did expensive custom-built log cabins, straw-bale homes, and mobile homes of farm laborers who nurtured harvests from the land, made rich by the interlocking irrigation ditches. Towering above the canyon was the Sleeping Ute Mountain, a behemoth that rose 9,977 feet and, from a distance, resembled the profile of an Indian chief, headdress to toe, sleeping on his back.

The bus stopped, and sixth grader Hoshi climbed aboard wearing oversized jeans and a dark shirt. He made his way to the back of the bus, where Shane enthusiastically greeted his older classmate.

"Hi, Hoshi! Long time no see!"

"Hello," Hoshi responded. He silently sat in one of the last seats of the bus and looked out the window.

The bus stopped four more times, rumbling past apple and peach orchards, and picked up several more children, including two tiny blond-haired brothers, Tim and Staton. Their shirtless father, Chris, stood with his young sons at the end of a gravel road that led to their farmhouse just over a mile away.

Debbie guided the bus to one of its final stops, a lonely-looking house that sat just off the road. She had stopped at the home of Harold, another sixth grader.

"Is he coming to Battle Rock this year?" she asked her passengers, hollering over the rattle of the bus windows.

"Yes, he's coming," Kayla yelled back.

There was no Harold, so she picked up the two-way radio that sat on the dashboard and called the school district. A disembodied voice told Debbie above the radio's crackle that Harold was indeed enrolled in Battle Rock this year. The radio was a necessity in this far-flung school district, where school buses traveled 2,087 miles a day, across canyon lands, through valleys, up mountainsides and down again. As bus no. 9 idled in front of Harold's house, Debbie peered through the cedar trees and honked twice. No one appeared. So with a couple of lurches, she steered the bus back onto the blacktop road. Turning from the canyon's beauty, I realized from the tittering of children's voices that the bus was fairly full. But when I surveyed my fellow passengers, I saw only one or two. Most of the children were so small they disappeared behind the backs of the seats. When the bus hit a bump, the tops of their heads, sometimes full faces, popped into view.

Thirty minutes after beginning our descent into the canyon, Debbie came to a stop in the parking lot. The children ran from the bus to join the other children on the playground, who had been brought to school by their parents. Moments later, Stephen appeared on the steps of the school with a handheld brass bell and gave it several rings; its musical clang carried on the wind. The students ran toward the school from every direction of the Sticker Patch, the name given to the playground because of the abundance of goat-head weeds. The children bounded up the steps and spilled into the classroom, along with seven parents who also came on the first day of school.

Stephen quickly launched into the morning, which included a tour for the children of the two-acre school grounds. Safety was the theme. Off-limits was the Battle Rock Cemetery, which sat next to the school and where many of McElmo Canyon's founding citizens rested amid askew headstones, native grasses, and purple and yellow wildflowers. Nor was anyone allowed near the ditch, the six-foot-deep irrigation canal that ran next to the school.

"Stay behind the fence," the teacher told his students.

"If you fell in, you would pwobably fwoat," said Troy, a tiny first grader who early in the school year established himself as the one student Stephen could always count on to render an opinion on the topic at hand.

"I'm sure you would float," the teacher told the boy, "but we don't want to take that chance. You older kids watch out for the younger ones."

The children were banned from getting too close to the propane tank that sat at the edge of the Sticker Patch and from climbing the Slick Rock, the smooth sloping canyon wall located behind the school. The students listened dutifully until one of them spotted movement. Two coyotes, partially hidden by the trees and boulders, navigated the Slick Rock with ease. The children oohed and ahed.

"Good eye!" Stephen exclaimed, coming to the end of the tour as the coyotes leaped over some small boulders and disappeared into a tangle of shrubs and trees.

*I*nside the school, with the parents gone, the teacher took an unencumbered view of the children whose triumphs and failures would, over time, become his own. As he surveyed the schoolroom, it bustled with commotion.

I took my place in a tiny chair at the third-grade table and was soon joined by Tim, a wiry boy with piercing blue eyes and short blond hair, who took the chair next to mine. Stephen and his aide, Teresa Blakney, passed out large plastic bins that held the children's notebooks and writing paper, crayons and colored pencils. Tim's little brother, Staton, whose blond hair was also trimmed short, put his supplies in his cubby, as the children called the bins, and took his place at the first-grade table.

Near the brothers sat Harold, the sixth-grade boy who hadn't been at his home earlier because his father had dropped him off. The bubbly, blond-haired boy, whose glasses always seemed to slip to the edge of his nose, had attended Battle Rock for six years. He had blossomed under Stephen's tutelage, but he still drifted in long stretches during the school day. At the start of the school year, Stephen sat Harold down for a heart-to-heart talk, telling him he had to become more focused if he was going to have a good experience at Cortez Middle School.

The teacher had a soft spot for Harold and the tiny blond-haired brothers, as he did for Kayla. She was his model student. She almost always finished her work before anyone else in the sixth grade. She aspired to be a writer for *Time* magazine and already had contributed several articles to the Cortez newspaper about local landmarks and school field trips.

As her classmates used construction paper to decorate their cubbies, Kayla, whose delicate features were framed by soft, shoulder-length brown hair, took a white sheet of paper and carefully drew the three crosses of Calvary. She wrote her name with a flourish and then taped her name tag to the front of her bin. She often wore T-shirts that bore Bible verses and the name of the Missionettes, an organization for children in the Assembly of God church, where her parents were members. Stephen wondered how she would adapt to home schooling, which her parents had already decided to do when she entered the seventh grade.

But the teacher was getting ahead of himself. As quickly as the day began, it was over. Stephen had a thankful look on his face. That he still taught at the school and that the school itself was still open were nothing short of miracles.

Chapter 2

No Ordinary School

*I*n *the early months of the school year,* Stephen watched the weather closely. The Indian summer slowly began fading in October as occasional frosts announced the advancing winter, and the teacher noticed the cottonwood trees dotting the canyon floor and the scrub oak trees on the Sleeping Ute Mountain turning bright yellow, gold, and crimson. I watched the trees turn their blazing shades and considered it art; it was as if a painter had dappled paint on the long mountain ridge. I made the trip to the canyon dozens of times and never once tired of taking in the mountain's seasonal change. But I soon discerned there were more practical reasons for Stephen's attention to the weather.

The winter storms that sometimes descended quickly on McElmo Canyon would soon make long nature tours impossible, and so he stuffed the fall weeks with several hikes that included Battle Rock's traditional ascent of the nearly eight-hundred-foot-tall Slick Rock. On one radiant fall afternoon, when the canyon walls shimmered under a full sun, Stephen suddenly left the classroom and then surprised everyone when he reappeared with several hundred feet of thick rope slung over one of his shoulders. I wasn't sure what the teacher had planned, but I heard the bad news soon enough.

"Okay, guys, we're going to climb the canyon," he announced.

Most of the children responded with enthusiasm; some groaned. Others looked terrified. He turned to me and said, "You can help when we get to the steep part." Stephen's request didn't interest me in the least. Nor did he wait for my answer, which would have been "no." Not at all sure scaling a canyon wall was a good idea for an out-of-shape forty-something guy who smoked, I nonetheless found myself walking toward the canyon's base, following Stephen and surrounded by the children. My reservations vanished as we took in the sweet aroma of the cedar and juniper trees that grew behind the school. We trekked past Spy Rock, so named because the cluster of boulders created a small chamber that allowed the smallest students to sit inside and watch the playground without being observed. Other students called the clump of boulders Butt Rock for obvious reasons.

As we continued the hike, I stumbled and fell on the rock-strewn path. My left knee, already weakened from a spill I had taken years earlier, broke the fall. Several of the children laughed, but there were some good Samaritans who steadied me as I picked myself off the ground.

As I limped toward the canyon wall, the gentle slope disappeared and the terrain rose sharply. Stephen wrapped a long, white rope around his waist and tied the other end to a rock at the bottom of the incline, creating a wobbly handhold for the children. I stood at the bottom with my aching knee to steady the rope.

"Everyone be very careful," he warned.

As he stood on the steep incline of the canyon wall, he looked down at the children and me, gathered about a dozen feet below. Their cheeks were flushed, and beads of perspiration had collected on the foreheads of some. I was out of breath and sweating profusely. The children formed a line, then waited to pull themselves up the wall one by one.

"Go as slow as you need to. You bigger kids watch out for the younger ones," Stephen told the children.

Almost immediately, Troy let go of the rope and began running across the Slick Rock.

"Come back here," Stephen yelled.

The boy scampered across the rock and then back to the rope, greeted by a stern gaze from the teacher, who could deliver the most withering of looks to recalcitrant students. But the perpetually good-humored Troy was oblivious to Stephen's silent rebuke. Truth be told, the first grader would have made a mountain goat proud.

Troy wasn't the only surefooted student at the school. Many of his classmates had grown up playing on the incline of the canyon wall and walked it just as an urban child rode a skateboard. But the rope was necessary for safety reasons and because of the school's changing population; several of the children, new to the school, were from cities and had never made the trek. Their only other experience going that high in the sky was riding an elevator up a skyscraper or riding a giant Ferris wheel. Halfway up the canyon wall, I wished I had stayed behind. I disliked heights, particularly when there was nothing to grasp besides a thick rope. Despite the deliberate slowness of the climb and the teacher's reassurance, Edna, a chubby first grader, froze out of fear. Tears welled in her eyes. Next came the wails. Such days were heavy lifting for Stephen, but he preferred a sobbing child on the side of a canyon wall to the other challenges he had faced in his years at the school.

*S*tephen was fired at the end of his first year. The circumstances that led to his dismissal all seemed a bad dream now, but in 1994 a lethal mix of events and personalities conspired

against the ponytailed teacher in ways he could not have anticipated. Teachers are easy targets in any school, but they are especially so in a rural community where they are very public
figures and are blamed for everything that goes wrong, even if
others create the issues. So it was with Stephen, who character-
ized his first year at Battle Rock very simply.

"I've been through the wars," he told me one afternoon at
school after his students were gone. Over the course of several
months, in quiet conversations at the school or while riding with
me to school board meetings, he reconstructed his six years at
Battle Rock. After each of our conversations, I wondered why he
still taught at the school.

Stephen's story had more twists and turns than the canyon
road he drove every day to get to school. His tenure began when
Audrey Allmon, his predecessor and a local icon, retired. When
she left the school, retiring after nearly a half century of teaching, most of that time at Battle Rock, the school district lopped off
the top three grades and sent the older children to schools in
Cortez. Audrey had saved the school from closing three times in
her storied thirty-six-year run at Battle Rock, arguing to school
district officials that the poorly graded gravel road was a dangerous commute into Cortez for the canyon's children in heavy rain
and snow. The road did have a long history of washing out, but it
was completely paved by the early 1990s. And now with Audrey
gone, McElmo Canyon parents fretted that the district would
close the school. They worried for good reason. Compared with
traditional public schools, Battle Rock was a relic and, to some
Cortez school administrators, a luxury.

Stephen stepped into the void. Drafted by McElmo parents,
Stephen researched and wrote a charter school proposal at night
in his Cortez home, after his day jobs as a carpenter and home-
builder and substitute teacher in the nearby town of Dolores. Ultimately approved by the local school district, the charter
allowed Battle Rock to remain open and operate independently
of the district while receiving financial support from school offi-

cials. The proliferation of charter school laws across the country—Colorado was in 1993 among the first states to pass such legislation—was intended to aid sputtering schools by encouraging novel approaches to education. The legislation was never intended to save one-room schools from closing. But McElmo Canyon residents, desperate to keep theirs open, knew a good deal when they saw one.

Now jealousies over Battle Rock Charter School flared when its new status generated a story on *NBC Nightly News*. Some town teachers grumbled openly and loudly about Stephen's smaller class size and about his $35,000-a-year salary. The attacks even became personal, some of the people in town remarking, "That old hippie, what does he think he's doing down there?"

"I told them that they weren't the groundskeeper, the secretary, the administrator, the janitor, all rolled into one," he told me on another occasion in defense of his salary.

Some of the antagonism reflected the dim view that many Cortezians took of the canyon. Many town folk considered canyon residents a strange breed—perceptions fueled in part by the occasional fisticuffs and gunfights that had erupted over the years between some longtime residents to settle disputes. When I asked Cortez residents about McElmo Canyon, their eyebrows arched and their responses carried a common theme: McElmo Canyon is a place filled with odd people who are even more closed than Cortezians to outsiders and change. Stephen was aware of the canyon's reputation, but he was still stunned in his first year at the school when McElmo residents turned on him. The teacher had no ready response.

The turmoil began when he started pushing reforms in a school unaccustomed both to the changes and to the speed with which he introduced them. His campaign earned him enemies among the longtime canyon families. Rural residents considered the school theirs, a member of the family. Battle Rock, in their minds, needed no fixing.

They tightly embraced the school and all its tradition, pushing back changes when they were proposed. The farm and ranch families didn't lose many battles over the years, but in 1986 they got a glimpse of a future they did not like. A California parent, the first of many outsiders who invaded McElmo Canyon in greater numbers in the 1990s, wanted to replace the school's outhouses with modern bathrooms. Sheldon Zwicker, a member of one of the canyon's most prominent families, was vehemently opposed. The outhouses worked just fine, and maybe, Sheldon argued one night at a school board meeting, they were an important introduction to rural life for city children. But Dick Stacy, the urban parent from California who had two children in the school, wanted modern bathrooms. He was unrelenting about it.

One afternoon, while I was in the school, Stephen summoned me to the cloakroom to meet the legendary Dick Stacy. He had left the area long before but had returned for a visit and wanted to see the school. He recalled the battle over bathrooms that was, I gathered, the first of many skirmishes between urban and rural families over control of the school. "We needed those bathrooms," he told me. "It's as simple as that."

Dick Stacy ultimately won his campaign in the name of sanitation and modernization, but he remembered receiving a call at home from Sheldon Zwicker. The rancher, who told me he considered Dick "a radical troublemaker," invited Dick to come to the school one evening to discuss standards for bathrooms. Dick Stacy wisely declined.

"I said, 'Sheldon, up your ass,'" recalled Dick Stacy, who then hung up the phone. "That's the last time I ever heard from Sheldon Zwicker." Sheldon too, all these years later, remembered the bathroom wars well. "To be honest, I was going to punch him out and throw him in the ditch."

When Stephen took over in 1994, Battle Rock had new bathrooms, but little else at the school had changed. Some students disappeared for weeks at a time to help with harvests and spring plantings, cattle drives, and hunting. School absences piled up at the canyon school, as well as the schools in town. These absences were nothing new in a rural area, but the school district became so concerned with the problem that it finally, and with some success, stemmed the absences by building in "floating holidays" that coincided with hunting seasons.

There were economic reasons for the absences. For many in Montezuma County, the elk and deer harvested during hunting season added significantly to some poor families' diets. So imbedded were hunting seasons in the local culture that KRTZ-FM, a local radio station, twice daily aired through its Buckskin Network announcements from families across the country trying to send messages to husbands, fathers, and brothers who had come to hunt the rich Four Corners region. Local stores advertised "hunter's specials," and the local newspaper often ran photos of hunters visiting Cortez. I neither hunted nor liked game, but I couldn't escape the local culture. On one weekday afternoon I walked to downtown Cortez to get a haircut and found the shop closed."Gone Hunting," said a note taped to the glass door.

Stephen knew about the local hunting culture and the unyielding worship of the agricultural calendar, but when students returned, many of them were impossibly behind in their studies. Their grades reflected their absences, of course, but that didn't stop parents from grumbling to Stephen that their children weren't learning anything—not math, not English, not history.

"How could I fill in weeks' worth of lessons in a few days?" he asked me one day at his home. He was amazed that parents expected, and demanded, the impossible. Parents accused him of being a poor teacher, of being insensitive to students, of not understanding rural life—of just about every sin a teacher could commit. On these issues, Stephen said little. More often than not, he simply acquiesced. Why bother, he thought, in causing a war of words steeped in the murky world of perception.

"I was trying to change and improve the school, and they didn't like it," he told me one afternoon after he talked about his early years at Battle Rock. "The school was circa 1900 when I got here, and they would have liked it to stay that way. I was a divisive force here. I didn't think I belonged. I was like a deer caught in the headlights."

McElmo Canyon residents didn't seem to care that some rural traditions, including those in country schools, needed updating, that there were now better and more efficient ways to live. Embracing tradition long after better ways arrived somehow fortified the families against the grittiness of rural life. As sure as the sun rose above the La Plata Mountains and sank behind the Sleeping Ute Mountain, rural families banked on the decades-old heritage of Battle Rock, down to the arrangement of the school's desks. When Stephen attended education conferences in Denver, he returned to find the school's old wood desks returned to the straight, military-like lines, instead of the cluster of desks he had created to group students by grade and ability. For all these transgressions, his contract was not renewed. Put more simply, he was fired.

Two weeks before school began, the school board, unable to find a replacement, asked Stephen to return. He wasn't sure he wanted the job, but he figured teachers needed to eat, too. Maybe the last of the turmoil had been wrung from the school, he thought. But the friction between change and tradition, urban and rural, still churning below the surface, erupted with even more force when, in 1997, Stephen hired local artist Sonja Horoshko as a teacher and art instructor.

Sonja had worse luck than Stephen. She angered Sheldon Zwicker after she admonished one of his sons for killing the insects on the Sticker Patch. Sonja had created the Battle Rock Bug Club to study the canyon's variety of insects, but Sheldon would have none of it. "Out here in the country, we destroy weaker animals, kill predators, kill weeds," he said, recalling some of the basis for the discord. "It's a matter of survival."

Ants held a special place on the Zwicker family's list of pests. "When my son was an infant, he wandered off as kids will sometimes do, and soon we heard him crying. By the time I got to him, I counted twenty-seven ant bites. Then the teacher aide scolded

my son for killing ants," Sheldon recalled. So it went without further explanation that ants were to be killed.

Sonja, a single woman who had relocated to Cortez from Denver two years before, wondered how she was supposed to know
family history and be familiar with rural mores about life and
death. But the next thing she knew, a protective fence erected
around an ant hill on the Sticker Patch was demolished. No one
owned up to destroying the fence, but the message was clear.
The Battle Rock Bug Club was quietly disbanded.

The bug incident paled in comparison, however, when the next
battle began brewing, and it would serve as the last stand for the
rural families. An art book with an illustration of Sandro Botticelli's 1485 masterpiece, *The Birth of Venus,* stunned a parent
who visited the school one day. Sonja had brought the reference
book from home and put it in the teacherage, out of sight of the
children but not from a parent's keen eyes. Breasts peeking out
from Venus's hands and her exposed thighs were simply too
much. Storm clouds gathered after the parent told others about
the nudity he found at Battle Rock. At least that's how the rural
and religious families saw it. The painting is, of course, one of
the world's most recognized masterpieces, but not to McElmo
Canyon's rural families, some of them belonging to a fundamentalist congregation so closed that few outside the church knew
what it believed in, besides relegating wives and daughters to
subservient roles. Most of the community in time called the conservative religious people "the Cult."

"I called my friends in Denver to tell them what was happening, and they didn't believe me," Sonja said. "They'd say, 'Oh,
you're imagining this,' or 'You're overreacting.'"

Sonja apologized to the parent who saw the book. So did
Stephen. They kept thinking the grumbling would disappear, but
it didn't. Venus only got bigger and bigger, like the real storm
clouds that sometimes gathered over the canyon and then ex-
ploded with a fury. When the school board considered her contract in what amounted to a vote of confidence, she survived by a

single ballot. After the vote, a school board member who was a
member of the fundamentalist group resigned after he failed to
oust Sonja. Within the week, the man and his two children were
gone.

That Sonja survived the vote on her contract and that one of
her biggest critics had resigned from the school board should
have ended the ruckus. In all likelihood the din over 512-year-old
Italian breasts and thighs would have at least ebbed had it not
been for the school board president dismissing another concerned parent's question about Venus with a flippant answer.

"Let's go on to something serious," the board president said
one night at a Battle Rock board meeting shortly after Sonja had
dodged the bullet. The next day, the parent pulled his four children out of the school, and the exodus was on. Early one morning, before Sonja left for school, Stephen called her at home to
tell her that other parents had taken their children out of Battle
Rock and more were threatening to do so. Sonja drove to
McElmo Canyon from her Cortez home, and when she was
halfway there, tears began rolling down her face. "I can't do this
anymore," she thought, as she made her way through the brown
landscape of a brisk November morning. She prayed and then let
go of all the angst, not at all sure what was next.

All told, thirteen children, half the school's enrollment, were
yanked from the school by their parents. Battle Rock had the financial wind knocked out of it when, to reflect the lower enrollment, the school district sliced the school's budget by nearly 50
percent. The two teachers were close friends, but Stephen was
nonetheless forced to lay off Sonja from her $15,000-a-year job.

After the exodus, Battle Rock was nearly as quiet as the old
cemetery sitting next to the playground. Children were upset,
Stephen was numb, and the school spent the entire day watching
videos on the school television set. The local school system allowed Battle Rock to continue operating for the remainder of the
school year, but its enrollment had to grow by the following fall
or it would be closed.

The discord was a good, if unwelcome, news story. But it was a measure of the region's conservatism that the *Durango Herald*'s decision over whether to run a photograph of the Botticelli art created a maelstrom of its own. When the *Herald,* which is available in nearby Cortez, ultimately did run a photo of the classic painting on its front page, the religious and conservative families that populated southwest Colorado in great numbers lambasted the newspaper. In the aftermath of the Battle Rock controversy, one letter writer suggested that if Sonja Horoshko was teaching Battle Rock students about the Italian masters, then perhaps Durango public schools should hire her. His was a distinctly minority view.

Sonja's experiences underscored one of many truths about rural America, even today. Women had a more difficult time than men making their way here. Women with strong opinions were shunned and ridiculed. Sexism still had deep roots, and many locals still believed that the proper role for women was in the home. Sonja retreated to her Cortez home and pursued her art, eventually offering successful workshops and private lessons.

Three years after the Botticelli controversy and six years after Stephen was fired and rehired, Battle Rock was blessed by relative tranquility at the start of a new school year. But Stephen had told me he always felt a placid McElmo Canyon was a dangerous sign. There was something in the water, or in the air, or both, that rendered him and the school vulnerable. Either way, it was difficult to separate the identities and fortunes of the teacher and the one-room school. Battle Rock was Stephen Hanson, or was it the other way around?

*A*re you okay?" Stephen asked the wailing Edna, the first of two students who bailed out of the hike up the canyon wall.

Edna didn't answer, her throat full of cries and her cheeks now wet with the steady roll of tears. I stood behind her on the incline, finally having caught my breath. I held out my hand, and Edna grabbed it tightly.

"Do you want to go back to the school?" I asked.

She nodded yes.

"Thank God," I said under my breath.

Edna and I began our unsettled descent with, as it happened, her older sister, Tina.

The third grader sat on the edge of the incline where the students were assembled waiting to take their turns going up the canyon wall. Tina's fingers tightly grasped the flattened edge of an oddly shaped boulder. Her whole body trembled as tears rolled down her face. When Edna and I finally reached the point where her sister sat frozen, the three of us made our retreat carefully down the canyon wall. By the time we reached the level land of the Sticker Patch, their tears had dried, and I was glad to be on horizontal ground. The sisters joined the half dozen other children in the school, all of them urban transplants or too young, who had decided to play computer games or read quietly rather than climb the Slick Rock.

The hike was indeed a rigorous exercise, and such outings gave the school the feel of an Outward Bound program. For the children who completed the climb, the reward was a million-dollar view. Even from the Sticker Patch, where I stood watching Stephen and the children, the views were spectacular. At the summit stood Apple Core Rock, so named by the children because it resembled an eaten apple. Apple Core stood nearly twelve feet tall, and it dwarfed the students. Beyond the rock formation lay the prize: an eighteen-inch dinosaur bone imbedded in the pink sandstone.

The children looked like tiny ants from my vantage point on the canyon floor as they walked the edge. Stephen allowed the children to wander the flat rim, an advantage that afforded them views of the eight-hundred- to thousand-year-old ruins of Anasazi granaries and dwellings built into the depressions of the canyon walls. They could also see Battle Rock Mountain, the remnant of a prehistoric volcano from which the school drew its name. There were several versions of the mountain's history, the most popular one pitting the Ute and Navajo in battle. The canyon's rim also offered a nearly unfettered view of the majestic Sleeping Ute Mountain.

After thirty minutes, Stephen and the children began their descent, the teacher again using the thick rope to assist students down the steepest stretch. Once on more level land, the children bounded through the rough terrain, just like the coyotes they had seen the first day of school. In the years the teacher had taken his students up and down the canyon wall, he hadn't experienced a single accident. But the hike emphasized one thing as the group returned to the school. "It's outings like this," Stephen told me as I waited at the fence separating the Slick Rock from the playground, "that tell me how out of shape I am."

McElmo Canyon provided a rich laboratory for Battle Rock, but sometimes not even the outdoors could supply all the lessons children needed. The teacher scheduled a variety of field trips during the school year. For many of the children, these excursions marked the only time they ventured beyond the sometimes stultifying isolation of Montezuma County.

Chapter 3

Country Boys

In the early weeks of school, Battle Rock's rhythm settled into a blend of outdoor hikes, academics, and music and Spanish lessons. Before the children began their work, however, the day started with a school tradition nearly as old as climbing the canyon wall. One morning, Tim, the reed-thin third grader, walked to the front of the class for the school's Share Time, Battle Rock's version of show-and-tell.

"A bull snake ate one of our chicks," Tim told his classmates as he stood in front of the blackboard.

"What did you do with the snake? Did you kill it?" asked a classmate.

"Did you see the bull snake?" Stephen asked.

"Yes, it had a big lump in his throat," he said, and then, almost in unison, Tim and several classmates added, "That's where the chick was."

"We trapped it," the boy said, with all the nonchalance that came from living in the country.

"Bull snakes are good," said Stephen, standing at the back of the room, dressed in khaki shorts, a dark polo shirt, and tennis shoes. "They eat the odd chick, but it eats mice, rodents, and other snakes."

"Rattlesnakes, too!" added Troy.

One by one, children walked to the front of the class during Share Time to tell stories of lives entwined with the land. The stories also reflected the blend of children with rural roots and those who had come from cities. For every story about snakes, horses, and cows, there were an equal number about holiday trips to Los Angeles, Phoenix, and Denver. After Tim returned to his chair, he quietly continued his tales about wildlife to his third-grade classmates and me.

"A bald eagle swooped down one day and carried off one of our ducks," he told the table in hushed tones. "The eagle ripped its heart out. I saw it," Tim said, illustrating the duck's violent death by jerking an imaginary heart from his chest.

"Tim," said the teacher, looking at the boy, as another child shared her story about going to Durango for a shopping trip. Tim smiled and fell silent.

Tim's stories were revelations to his urban classmates, who raised their eyebrows at the story, but for the rural children the story was all part of life in the canyon. They had seen chickens, ducks, and small pets carried off by predators living in the cliffs and fissures of the canyon. Share Time was a glimpse into the children's rich lives, though some of the details they shared were better left unspoken. In years past, some children talked so quickly that they spilled the beginnings of what would have been embarrassing details from home had Stephen not stopped them. He knew the home situations of his students well, whose parents were in jail and whose parents had been stopped for driving while intoxicated. In the first thirty minutes of the school day, Battle Rock students recounted the full range of experiences, from life to death. One fall morning, Stephen somberly reported to the children that Troy's baby sister, suffering from a childhood disease, had died in surgery in a Minneapolis hospital. The children were uncharacteristically quiet the rest of the morning. There were few secrets in a rural community, and there were absolutely none in a one-room school as far as the children were concerned. They took their triumphs and reversals, along with those of their families, in stride.

Share Time ended promptly at 8:30 every morning, at which point Stephen pushed the children into the day's regimen, which included, literally, reading, writing, and arithmetic. As the children settled in for their first lessons, Staton, the pudgy first grader who was Tim's little brother, began his math sheet of twenty problems. Almost immediately, he struggled.

"What's 39 – 10?" he asked a classmate sitting across the table.

"You have to figure it out!" the fourth-grade boy replied.

"What is it?" Staton insisted.

The fourth grader, a stout boy with dark hair, rolled his eyes. He closed the book he was reading and walked around the table to help Staton. "Here, watch," he said as he helped his young classmate calculate the problem.

Staton navigated 15 – 10 and then considered 61 – 10. He was stumped again.

"How do I do this?" he asked.

The fourth grader looked at the boy and sighed heavily but got up from his chair and walked around the table to help Staton.

"One more, that's it. I'm done," Staton said, alternately sitting down and standing up to do his work. The next question required the boy to find an object in the classroom that was ten centimeters long. Without getting out of his chair or using a ruler he answered the question.

"My dog," he wrote.

"There, I'm finished," Staton said, putting his paper in a manila folder that held his schoolwork. He walked across the room, his black leather cowboy boots clacking on the hardwood floor, and selected a book about horses. Tim was deeply engrossed in his math as Staton stopped by to check his big brother's progress.

"Poor Tim," said Staton shaking his head as he looked at his brother's half-completed math worksheet. "Poor, poor Tim." Then Staton went to one of the two blue-cushioned chairs that were premium reading spots the children enjoyed only after Stephen granted permission. Staton sank into the deep cushions and lost himself in stories about mustangs, quarter horses, and palominos.

Tim didn't look happy as he worked through a more advanced sheet of addition and subtraction exercises. He looked at the problem, then held out his fingers on the table and counted or subtracted until he got the correct answer. Tim worked the problems methodically and quietly, as Stephen worked individually with other students on their worksheets.

Teresa, Stephen's assistant, walked with stealthy silence among the tables of fidgeting children. She inspected the math sheets to make sure they were complete. Teresa then checked the papers and recorded the grades. She was so quiet as she walked among the students that she surprised sixth graders Hoshi and Harold. They were telling jokes.

"Do your work," she ordered. Their smiles vanished, and they picked up their pencils.

"Stat, you haven't finished your math work," said Teresa, after she stopped and looked through Staton's math folder sitting on the table where he had been working. About a dozen problems were left unfinished. The boy, his legs draped over the armchair of the blue-cushioned chair, looked up from his book, perturbed.

"Come finish this paper now," Teresa said.

Staton closed his book and went back to the table, where he sat long faced and finished his work with a pained, furrowed brow. Across the room, Tim was still counting on his fingers as he neared completion of his math assignment.

Tim and Staton Jeter lived just over a mile off McElmo Canyon Road, down a narrow gravel lane that spanned a bridge. Bus no. 9 dropped the brothers off at a collection of weathered mailboxes, then they retrieved the bicycles they had concealed in the brush that morning and pedaled to their home. One afternoon, after the brothers had invited me to visit them, I gave them a ride home. We drove over the small, narrow bridge spanning McElmo Creek's brown water and down the gravel road that meandered by pastures of grazing cattle and horses. When we arrived at the eighty-year-old farmhouse where they lived, I followed them into the kitchen of the three-room house. We found their father, Chris Jeter, retrieving a large orange water cooler. He was a wiry man in his mid- to late twenties, with thinning hair and deep-blue eyes that often sparkled at his sons.

"Come on, boys," he said. "We need to get some water."

Tim, Staton, and I followed Chris into a thick twist of growth behind their house, toward the pink wall of the canyon, navigating a plank that spanned the five-foot-wide ditch. All three possessed great balance and walked across the plank with confidence, as if it were a wide sidewalk. By the time I had slowly made my way across the plank, they were several yards ahead. After hiking for just under five minutes, we arrived at a depression in the canyon wall. Here, deep in the brush, was a pristine spring that provided the family's drinking water. Big-city people all over the country paid good money for tiny bottles of pure spring water, the kind that the Jeters drew directly from Mother Nature. They had no alternative since their home had no running water. Chris had recently installed a septic tank as part of a plan to eventually install plumbing in their home. The project was on his "to do" list. Until the plumbing arrived, Chris and the boys trekked daily to the shimmering spring.

I had come to the Jeter home with great anticipation and curiosity, given all I had heard about the family. Urban expatriates and even some longtime rural neighbors viewed the family as odd, living a lifestyle that was more difficult than it had to be in 1999. Although the family lived in a weather-worn farmhouse with an outhouse a few feet outside the back door, the Jeters weren't alone in their rudimentary lifestyle. Many Montezuma County residents still lived unvarnished lives without running water, indoor plumbing, central air and heat, or washers and dryers. Cortez's several Laundromats were often jammed in the evenings with families whose lifestyles were a stark contrast to those of some of their new urban neighbors, who had all the modern conveniences. But for the Jeters, and many other rural families, less was more.

Chris was well aware of what urban people thought of how his family lived, and he had heard via the canyon's very healthy grapevine all the condescending comments by his canyon neighbors. He didn't wait for me to ask about the family's lifestyle, directly addressing McElmo Canyon's wagging tongues.

"People say we don't have anything, that we don't have indoor plumbing, that we're poor," he volunteered as he filled the cooler. "I've heard all the comments. But hey, we're living."

The Jeters may have been poor, but Stephen told me early in the fall that he thought Tim and Staton lived lives richer than any of his other students. After spending an afternoon and evening with the boys and their parents, I agreed. The treks to the spring for drinking water were only a small part of what made their lives so extraordinary, even by McElmo Canyon's rustic standards.

The canyon floor was strewn with Anasazi ruins and artifacts, from granaries to whole pots and drinking vessels. Many of the region's ancient artifacts were exhibited at regional museums, but Tim and Staton didn't have to travel beyond the family's spring to consider the canyon's pre-Columbian history. Chris told us that Anasazi paintings had once decorated the canyon wall above the spring, according to old-timers who had seen the prehistoric art decades earlier. We looked at the canyon wall above the spring, but the ancient drawings had long disappeared, forever lost to the moisture.

All of us took long drinks of that cool water, using an old tin cup sitting near the spring. Then with Chris carrying the full cooler, we made our way back to the house, where the boys began feeding the family's livestock.

Tim watered the three hogs standing in the middle of a muddy stall that was already littered with scraps of squash, corn, and other leftovers from the family's dinner table. Nearby, a partially submerged carcass of a rooster that had died from disease floated in the mud and half-eaten vegetables. A pig pushed the rooster with its nose, took a bite, and grunted. "A pig will eat anything," Chris said to me. I looked at the filthy pig devouring the decomposing rooster and reconsidered pork chops.

As the pigs cavorted in the mud, Tim began filling their water bucket. He put one end of a long green hose in the gurgling irrigation ditch that ran a few feet away and a couple of feet higher than the pen. He then put the other end in a water bucket. Gravity did the rest as water flowed downhill through the hose and began filling the bucket, which the pigs promptly stepped into and overturned.

"Oh, man!" Tim exclaimed, as he jumped the rickety wire fence of the pig pen, into the messy mix of table scraps, ankle-deep mud, and three thirsty pigs. He righted the tub and water began filling it again. This time the pigs stood back a bit until the tub was filled, perhaps sensing that they were pressing their luck if they overturned the tub again.

The boys worked hard at "choring," as they called these tasks, but they played just as hard. Once they had fed and watered the pigs, the boys climbed on their horses, a tan quarter horse named Rena May and a spotted pony named Shawnee, and galloped bareback through a field of wild grass and alfalfa. I followed on foot and almost immediately sank ankle deep into the field's mud. Recent rains had transformed the pasture into mush. As I extricated my tennis shoes from the muck, Princess, Tim's light-brown pet calf, galloped past me after the boys. Tim and Staton raced each other across the field, galloping on their horses, and leaving me standing in the field. Their "backyard" was an immense pasture framed by the canyon wall and the gravel road we had driven earlier that afternoon. Now, bored with horseback riding, Staton galloped up to me and announced that he wanted some fruit.

"You want some plums?" Staton asked me.

"Sure," I said.

"They're over there," he said, getting off his horse.

He pointed to a tangled thicket of trees that grew at the pasture's edge. There was no point of entry to the thicket, at least none that I could see. We walked to the trees, and Staton parted several low-lying branches to expose an impossibly narrow path. I soon found myself prone, crawling along the wet ground. Staton never once had to bend over to clear the branches of the thick bushes and willow that fed off the water from the nearby ditch. Sometimes the dense growth hung so low that Tim, not quite five feet tall, dropped on all fours to maneuver the path the boys had created from their numerous trips to the wild plum trees.

"Watch out for snakes," Staton yelled over his shoulder to me.

"Oh?" I said. "What kind?"

"Big ones," Staton replied.

I slithered faster along the ground, and Staton held up a bunch of willows and then let them go too soon. They stung my face, and I made a promise that the next time I desired plums I would take myself to the grocery store.

"Sorry, Bill," Staton said.

"No problem," I replied, spitting out bits of leaves.

After what seemed an eternity, we reached the center of the thicket, my shirt muddy and torn and my canvas tennis shoes now completely covered in mud. As I straightened my six-foot frame, I marveled at my surroundings. I stood under a canopy of wild vines and tree branches so dense that the light inside the clearing was dim. The quarter-sized plums, warmed by the filtered sun, were sweet and plump, some of them so fat that they burst at the seams. Staton pushed away the feeding honeybees and picked a plum. He turned with a smile and, with mud-encased fingers, handed me the fruit.

This was no time to be squeamish. I put the plum in my mouth, bit it in half, and the fruit's bittersweet juices coated my mouth. The grocery store didn't have fruit this good. I gleaned the fruit from the uppermost branches that the boys couldn't reach, and we feasted until we had eaten all the plums that hadn't been chewed up by the bees. We emerged from the thicket, our lips sticky from the plum syrup, to hear the boys' mother calling out over the pasture in a tone that said she meant business. She had arrived from town, where she managed the city's animal shelter.

"You boys come finish your chores," Andrea hollered from the back door of their home. Her strong voice drifted over the pasture to the boys. Their smiles disappeared, and we quickly made our way back to the house, where Andrea, hands on her hips, waited to issue a list of verbal orders.

"Go unload my truck of the groceries and bring them in. Chris, did you get water? What happened here?" she asked, looking at the floor.

She stood in the middle of her kitchen and peered at a trail of milk leading from the kitchen trash, across the floor, to a garbage can outside, evidence that whoever had emptied the trash had been less than careful. Chris studied the floor and looked out the door at the trail.

"I dunno what that is," Chris said, shrugging.

"I don't know," Tim said. But the boy knew very well what the white liquid was since he had emptied the trash. One only admitted so much wrongdoing to Andrea.

She was a pretty woman whose demeanor suggested someone much older than her twenty-four years. "There's never time to clean a house right when you live on a ranch," she said to me, looking at her overflowing sink as she unpacked the first of several grocery bags in her kitchen. She spoke the truth. A large bin of vegetables sat in the sink, on top of dishes and glasses from the night before. Dishes were washed after Andrea heated water in two large pans on the stove.

"She heats the water for dishes at night, and in the morning, they're still dirty," Chris offered with a smile, reappearing at the open back door with the last of the groceries.

"Things get done when they get done," Andrea retorted, squeezing some of her purchases into the refrigerator and the cabinets, now overstuffed with food, including her canned jams and jellies and vegetables from fall harvests. Chris smiled.

The boys finished feeding the months-old chickens, one batch in the coop, another in a small wire pen in the front yard. The family might have had more young chickens had the boys secured the gate to the coop. They didn't, and the resulting carnage offered Tim a chance to stand before the class during Share Time to tell his classmates about a marauding bull snake. The chicks that weren't eaten by the snake were finished off that same morning by the many puppies Andrea had brought home to raise before taking them back for adoption at the animal shelter. The day wasn't a good one for the chicks or Andrea, who had counted on the chicks to produce eggs and fryers. She was upset, but she never stayed angry for long.

"You have to have a tough stomach to live out in the country," she told me in a direct tone. She would get no argument from me. It had only been an hour ago that I had seen the pig enjoying a rooster dinner.

She had a steely, no-nonsense disposition when it came to managing the acreage she and Chris leased from family and the Bureau of Land Management, but she had a soft core that explained in large part how she came to be Tim's mother. With the boys outside working, she told me she had lived with Tim's father in Grand Junction, 204 miles north of McElmo Canyon, and the fallout from their relationship and Grand Junction's booming growth forced her hand. She had to get to a more peaceful place, and the country was the antidote for a life she saw unfolding for herself—one she did not want. Not in Grand Junction, which was as close to a city as she ever wanted to get. She wasn't Tim's biological mother, but after five years of fighting social service agencies, she won custody of Tim.

"The social service worker told me, 'You're nineteen and single, and you have two jobs, and why do you want this boy?'" Andrea recalled. "I said, 'Are you kidding? Who else has raised this boy? Where is his mother? Where is his father? I am the only mother this child has had. I have raised him.' I couldn't believe someone in child protective services could say something like that to me."

So not yet twenty, Andrea found herself with her own son, Staton, and then Tim and living with relations in Durango, where she worked a series of jobs at veterinarian clinics and animal shelters. One day, one of Chris's cousins who knew Andrea put the two together. He knew Chris liked horses and that Andrea liked horses, and thought the two would like each other. They did. They married in the summer of 1999 and moved into the house with no running water, owned by one of Chris's aunts. Andrea couldn't have been happier.

She made jams from wild grapes growing on Chris's aunt's land, canned tomatoes, squash, and zucchini, and raised rabbits and chickens for the family dinner table. She kept the family of four on an even and loving keel, despite the chaos sometimes created by Tim and Staton.

Chris and Andrea walked outdoors to inspect the beginnings of a larger chicken coop that Chris was building, while the boys and I moved to the living room to watch a video. From the corner of the sofa where I was sitting, I heard several puppies growling. I went into the kitchen, and in that moment, I was glad for Tim and Staton that their mother was outdoors. One of them had left a bag of groceries on the floor, which escaped Andrea's eye for order, and the puppies came through the open back door and broke into several packages of hamburger meat. I alerted the boys, and Staton came to the kitchen and saw the now-empty packages on the kitchen floor. He picked them up, threw them in the trash can, and returned to the sofa. No one bothered to tell Andrea.

After a dinner of fried chicken, baked beans, and coleslaw, the family gathered to see Tim's latest archeological find. The boy produced an ornate piece of Anasazi pottery he had found outside the back door. The shard had elaborate stick figures, or maybe it was writing.

"This is very rare, Tim!" exclaimed Andrea, who, on top of everything else she did, was an amateur Anasazi expert. "It's not every day you find pottery with writing on it."

Chris offered that the shard was probably part of a ceremonial cup. Tim was pleased and put it back in an old cigar box where he kept dozens of other shards he had found in the yard and along the base of the canyon wall that ran behind the Jeter home.

The boys retreated to the family's television set to continue watching their video, while Chris, Andrea, and I moved to lawn chairs outside. The setting sun silhouetted the canyon rim, and as the last rays disappeared behind the ragged outcroppings, the canyon floor was illuminated by dozens of lights pouring out from homes that dotted the land.

"You used to be able to sit out here and not see a single light," said Chris, bundling up in a blue denim jacket against the night's pressing chill.

"It's all the outsiders coming in," said Andrea.

"I wish they would all go back from where they came," said Chris.

Their lament was one I heard often in Montezuma County. Neither had ever lived in a real city, and they weren't aware, or willing to concede, that growth also brought, more often than not, jobs. More porch lights seemed like a small trade-off to me given all the grousing I had already heard about people wanting and needing employment. No one said anything more about how the canyon was changing; the night was too beautiful, and our discussion returned to more basic matters.

The hour was too late, and the night too cold, to take baths. The Jeters often took theirs in the morning at Chris's aunt's home, located across the pasture and beyond the wild plum trees.

"It would be nice to have running water and be able to take a hot shower," Andrea started, as Chris finished her sentence: "especially on days when you have to feed the cattle in the cold rain or snow and you come in chilled to the bone. A hot shower would help."

Andrea told me that they could afford to live in town, had the financial wherewithal to do so, "but then I would have to give up all of this," she said, spreading her arms toward the land she and Chris were working and, above, to a brilliant exhibition of shooting stars.

"No thanks," she said. "I'll stay here."

The night sky was difficult to fully appreciate in cities, with all their lights. But in McElmo Canyon, the heavens were so brilliant that people often sat in lawn chairs and looked at the sky until their necks hurt, which is what we did on that chilly autumn night.

Chapter 4

A Fitful Transition

Cortez cast a long shadow over McElmo Canyon and the rest of Montezuma County for a single reason. In the West, where the distances are vast, where the nearest towns are fifty to seventy miles apart, sometimes further, Cortez's downtown stores were convenient. Main Street, like the town, was extraordinarily plain. There was little neon on storefronts, save for the façade of the historic art deco Fiesta Theater, Cortez's single movie house. The town might be forgiven. In a farm and ranch community, where crops and livestock demanded so much attention, aesthetics were an afterthought. So too, apparently, was decent housing.

When I arrived in the summer of 1999 to find a place, I quickly went through several choices, rejecting them all. One house leaned to the left, another tilted to the right. Crossed off my list was an apartment complex made of cinderblock that sat next to an industrial park. I also vetoed a mobile home that faced the town's sewage plant. After nearly a week, I found a one-bedroom cottage that fronted an alley. The dwelling sat at the back of a much larger house that was inhabited by an eighty-one-year-old man, who quoted me a rent of $200 a month. Even by a small town's standards, the rent was low. None of the floors was level, but the place was furnished with an ancient color television, a lumpy recliner, a foldout sofa, and a 1950s-style kitchen table with a tiny stove and refrigerator.

"You'll probably freeze in the morning when you take a shower," said Carl, the owner, as he showed me the tiny bathroom without heat. The cottage had most recently been home to a woman who had just died. The furniture had belonged to her, but Carl said I could use it if I didn't mind. I tried to remember why finding a home recently vacated by death sounded familiar, and then it came to me. When I first moved to New York City and still lived in free housing supplied to new employees by the *Times,* friends told me one way to find an apartment in Manhattan's tight housing market was to read the obituaries and then find out where the deceased lived. I passed on that suggestion and used a broker instead. But in Cortez, more than 2,000 miles from New York, I had succeeded, without even trying, in using a city-styled approach to find a place to live.

"There's one other thing," Carl told me as we concluded the tour of the four-room house. "My house is on the market, and you may have to move if it's sold."

"No problem," I said. Given everything I had seen, the cottage was by far my best option. Carl and I sealed the deal with a handshake.

"No lease, no deposit," Carl said when I asked. "I take a man at his word."

But just two months after settling in, Carl did sell his place, and I was on the move again. One Saturday, I walked across the lawn to Carl's garage sale. He gave me several items, including a forty-year-old fisherman's basket, the kind that Brad Pitt used in *A River Runs Through It.* I considered it a valuable consolation prize because a similar basket at an antique shop in the nearby town of Dolores carried a price tag of $70. Carl also introduced me to his son and daughter-in-law, who had come to help him move.

"This is Bill . . . Bill . . ." Carl said, trying to remember my last name. "This is Bill Sticks. He's from New York." Carl was hard of hearing, or had a poor memory, or both, possibilities I discerned early on when, after telling him my name repeatedly, he ended the conversation with "Well, have a nice day, Bob."

I ignored the odd look Carl's relatives gave me and didn't bother to correct my landlord. I had other issues to deal with, namely finding a new place to live.

Abandoning any sense of standards, I found a new residence a few blocks from Carl's cottage for $375 a month. The house leaned, and the floors were uneven. The windows in the bedroom were cracked and taped, and the single gas heater on the living room wall didn't begin to adequately warm the place. As the autumn turned colder, the wind rushed through the windows and under the front door. I complained, and the owner and her husband tacked heavy plastic over the windows. The coverings did little to correct the problem, and in heavy winds the flapping of plastic kept me awake. Two months later, I moved out after I came down with bronchitis.

My third home in five months was a decades-old farmhouse outside Cortez down a gravel road. For $325 a month, I had two bedrooms, a kitchen table, dishes, pots and pans, and propane heat. The house also came with the added bonus of a wood-burning stove in the kitchen that my new landlord promised "keeps the place toasty."

Finding decent housing was a rite of passage for every other newcomer I met, including John and Brenda Burns, a Los Angeles couple who sent two of their three children to Battle Rock. One night over dinner in their home, I listened to their introduction to Montezuma County, which had been every bit as challenging as mine.

"Either the houses were too small and dumps, or too expensive," said Brenda, describing their housing horrors. They ultimately settled on a small bungalow whose only source of heat, they were chagrined to learn, was a wood-burning stove. They found themselves gathering wood at night, in predawn hours, in the cold, and in the snow. They ultimately learned how much wood to collect, and they did it during the day, but banking the fire at night remained an unsolved mystery. They rousted themselves from sleep to keep the warmth going, and during the winter there was another problem that bothered Brenda, a fastidious housekeeper. The puddles of water created by snow melting off the wood drove her to distraction. She eventually learned to overlook the mess because there were other issues: the cost of keeping the home heated. A cord of wood wasn't cheap, and one autumn to save money the family decided to go to the mountains with new friends to chop their own.

"We went up to 10,000 feet, and it's beautiful. But there was no air," said Brenda, rolling her eyes. On that occasion, the family had found available wood near the tree line, and while chopping the trees, they had become faint because of the thin air. "You talk to the old-timers around here, and they spent the entire summer collecting wood."

Many of Cortez's homes were still heated by wood-burning stoves; the telltale signs were the plumes of gray smoke that rose from house after house. Urban families had no frame of reference for collecting wood, and families like the Burnses were consumed by it. Sometimes the task was simply beyond them, especially on a day when it was so cold no one wanted to venture outside to fill the empty woodbin. John and Brenda were both sick with colds and fever, and so they turned to Brenda's mother, Lana, who eventually joined them in Cortez after she too left Los Angeles. Brenda asked her mom to sacrifice one of her arts and crafts objects to the stove, a hearty piece of wood decorated with a painting of a rabbit. That first year in Cortez, the family was relieved when spring arrived. But the turn of seasons did not mean they were finished with their rudimentary heating system.

"One day I was outside and saw the chimney on fire," said

John. Alarmed at the sight, he quickly extinguished the flames with a hose, but another lesson was learned. "No one told us we had to clean the thing!"

Moving to Cortez hadn't been in the Burnses' plans. Just seven years earlier, the family was deep in a southern California lifestyle, living in the runaway sprawl that is greater Los Angeles, enjoying the Los Angeles Lakers, the museums, and the expansive malls. All that changed when an early 1990s recession grounded the state's soaring economy and, in a wave of layoffs by the Los Angeles Unified School District, John lost his job as a high school band director. He scrambled to find other jobs within a two-hour driving radius from their home, but dozens of people applied for every position he found.

As John waited to hear from school districts, another disaster loomed. The Burnses' home actually depreciated, as many single-family dwellings did in California's recession. The couple tried to sell, then rent their three-bedroom, two-bath home. Unable to do either, and to protect their credit, they returned their house to their mortgage lender. John and Brenda waited quietly for life to break their way, and it did so in an expected way. As their desperation deepened, John drove to Greeley, Colorado, for a job fair. The trip eventually produced calls from three school districts, but the one from the Dolores public schools near Cortez puzzled John.

"I didn't apply there," he told the voice on the telephone. John looked at a map and couldn't find Dolores in southwest Colorado. There was nothing in the southwest corner of Colorado, he thought, looking at the map, nothing at all, except Durango, and to the west of Durango, a tiny dot representing Cortez.

"Well, will you come anyway?" the voice from Dolores asked.

When he arrived in Dolores, he discovered that the Greeley job fair organizers had forwarded his résumé to several school districts beyond those to which he had applied. One of fifteen candidates, he interviewed for the Dolores position. When he returned to his Cortez motel, he explored the town, walking to the nearby Wal-Mart "because that was the only thing to do." Later that evening, he stood on his hotel balcony and took in the richness of Mesa Verde, which, translated from Spanish, means "green table." The folds of the mountain holds Mesa Verde National Park, which attracts 600,000 visitors every year to view the resplendent cliff dwellings. As John took in the wild terrain, he remembered thinking, "This is a neat place." Before returning to California, he accepted an offer from the Dolores school system.

"We're moving where?" Brenda asked when her husband phoned her with the good news.

"Cortez," John answered.

"Where's that? New Mexico? Arizona?"

"Colorado," John answered.

"Within the week," Brenda recalled, raising her eyebrows in disbelief, "we were in Cortez."

Small-town life wasn't what the couple expected. Locals weren't friendly, and the Lakers were rarely carried by local cable television. Cortez was just over a thousand miles from Los Angeles, and even further in temperament. But the Burnses dug in and started over in a town so isolated that even urban Coloradoans, if they knew Cortez at all, routinely placed it in New Mexico.

The geographic confusion was easy to understand. Cortez sits deep in the left corner of the state, just fifty miles from the Four Corners Monument, where a modest plaque marks the only spot in the country where four states, Colorado, New Mexico, Utah, and Arizona, share a common point. Beyond the town lay the vast painted deserts of the arid Southwest. There was no good reason for Cortez or Montezuma County to exist, at least early on, except that when the county was carved in 1888 from La

Plata County, now to the east, mapmakers had to draw county lines somewhere. A county needed a seat, of course, and the town of Cortez was born.

The new county was immense. It sprawled across 2,037 square miles, a land mass nearly twice the size of Rhode Island and half as big as Connecticut. Montezuma County was as remote as it was big. When the town was first plotted in 1886 in the county's geographic center, wagons hauling lumber for the first buildings couldn't even find Cortez. There were no street signs, no markers, nothing. And though Cortez was the seat, it wasn't even the county's preeminent community. In those early years, Dolores and Mancos, a small community east of Cortez, both enjoyed more prominence. The railroad ran through both towns, and Dolores had the added advantage of a river that ran along its business district. Cortez had neither a river nor a railroad. Cortezians, past and present, could blame the town's poor location on a group of well-intentioned Maine investors who founded Cortez simply as a supply center for miners already in the area.

Although precious metals were found in Montezuma County, the biggest hauls of gold and silver occurred to the east of Cortez in dozens of little camps that ultimately became bona fide communities, like the appropriately named town of Silverton. Montezuma's mining bust, along with the absence of a railroad and a river, set into motion Cortez's uneven economic life as the economy shifted to agriculture. But there was never enough rain or arable terrain for farmers, most of whom coaxed harvests with great difficulty. Water was hauled into the town by horse-drawn wagons from nearby towns whose founders had the presence of mind to build next to a source.

The completion of a water pipeline in 1888, coinciding with the creation of the new county, was an engineering marvel for the day and utterly changed the face of Cortez and Montezuma County. When it was finally completed, after horrendous cost overruns amid accusations of mismanagement, the *Montezuma Journal* celebrated by devoting a front-page article to the technological wonder, declaring in a headline over a curiously sparse, 282-word story: "Water! Completion of the Montezuma Tunnel. Welcome the Waters of the Dolores."

The 5,400-foot tunnel meant that, for the first time, farmers and ranchers were no longer forced to rely on divine providence for water. More than 200,000 acres of dry land were poised for irrigation from the Dolores River. Although water took some of the sting out of being bypassed by the railroad, there was no denying that life was still a hard go in frontier Montezuma County, beset by chronic doctor shortages and uneven medical care.

Life's harshness was reflected in the Battle Rock Cemetery, which sat next to Battle Rock school and whose playground served as the graveyard's right-of-way. Fully a third of the seventy-three graves in 1999 marked the resting places of McElmo Canyon infants and children. Many of the headstones were hand hewn from the canyon's sturdy sandstone and included comforting Bible scriptures and carvings of elk and deer, cattle and horses. Headstones that didn't commemorate brief lives marked the final stops for men and women who lived well into their eighties and nineties, underscoring two truths about life in rural America: surviving childhood or childbirth was no given, even through the middle of the twentieth century, and those early McElmo Canyon residents who survived both often enjoyed longevity from the rigorous, healthy lifestyles that came with working the land.

There was one bright spot in those bleak early years. Montezuma County's orchards, particularly those of McElmo Canyon, put the county on the map at the end of the nineteenth century. McElmo peaches won honors at Chicago's 1893 Columbian Exposition, which celebrated the five hundredth anniversary of Christopher Columbus's arrival to America and introduced the Ferris wheel and cotton candy. The fair also featured a one-third scale model of Battle Rock Mountain constructed in papier-mâché; cedar trees and boulders from Montezuma County were transported to the Chicago exhibit to give the mountain authenticity. The West was in vogue, and Montezuma County basked in the national limelight as never before. National headlines were generated again when McElmo peaches triumphed at the 1904 World's Fair in St. Louis. For years, the local newspaper devoted prominent space on its second page to the awards won by the county's peaches. There was little else to brag about in those early decades.

All that changed with the discovery in the 1950s of the Aneth oil field, a monstrous natural gas and oil operation that spread across the Navajo reservation. The population of Cortez nearly doubled, and the town's only bona fide economic boom of the twentieth century actually resulted in spendable income, and lots of it, for the first time in anyone's memory. The community enjoyed an unrivaled run of prosperity from the 1950s through the early 1960s. But the oil reserves were ultimately sucked from the red earth, and lacking the technology then that makes secondary recovery possible today from largely depleted oil and natural gas fields, the town was plunged into yet another economic free fall from which it never fully recovered.

Cortezians who tried to escape their luckless economy by attending the movies must have wondered in 1974 whether the world, or at least Hollywood, was against them. When the hit movie *Blazing Saddles* opened in town, so many Cortezians groused that the movie portrayed rural people as backwater simpletons that the film was pulled by the local theater after a short, problematic run.

If Hollywood agitated Cortez, *USA Today* riled the place when it described the town as ugly. The local paper ran an editorial decrying the article, and its letters column was jammed with correspondence from a bruised populace demanding an apology. None ever came, of course. A community could hold a mirror to its face and take an account. But it was quite another matter when someone else held the looking glass, especially when the portrayal was unflattering, and it almost always was when an outsider passed judgment. The local venom rose in proportion to who held the mirror, and it ran very high when "those damn Californians in Hollywood" or a national newspaper "back East" delivered the reviews. Cortezians could criticize their town, and they did so loudly and often, but outsiders better mind their damn business.

Despite the icy reception I received upon arriving, I largely avoided the backlash against outsiders because I enjoyed an entrée denied most newcomers. I was the guy from New York writing a book. I had also remembered from my years in small Texas towns to be friendly but don't go poking around. I didn't have to worry about digging for stories in Cortez or in McElmo Canyon; information was offered, often without my asking.

"People here act like they mind their own business," one resident told me. "But they call each other and gossip like mad."

Talk they did. Residents told me who had extramarital affairs, who had drinking problems, who had drug addictions, who had been arrested. These people, I noticed, never told stories about themselves. But I didn't have to worry about that, either. People who spilled embarrassing or unflattering details about others were in turn dissected themselves. When I shopped for groceries, went to the post office, even walked down Main Street, I often crossed paths with someone about whom I possessed knowledge of some personal blot. A lawyer could have made good money over slander cases.

Cortezians couldn't escape the fact that they contributed generously to the unfavorable reviews. One fall Saturday in 1996, the Montezuma County Child Advocacy group hosted hot air balloon rides to raise money, and an incident involving one of the balloons was vintage Cortez. As a hot air balloon with passengers floated over a pasture, a rancher fired on it with a .22-caliber rifle. The woman told police she was asleep in her tent when the balloon's propane blower awakened her, the local paper reported on its front page. She told officers that she fired on the balloon because she was afraid it would spook her cattle. Charges of

menacing with a deadly weapon, a Class 5 felony, were ultimately dropped at a subsequent court hearing. But the incident
spoke volumes about the mentality of the place, about the independence of people, their right to own guns, and their right to
use them when the occasion demanded.

The urban people who moved to Cortez in the 1990s shook
their heads at the town's seemingly boundless eccentricities.
They also admitted that the stories made good dinner conversation. When they told their city friends about life in the town, their
urban friends dismissed the stories. "No town could be that
weird," they responded. They hadn't been to Cortez.

But the town and the county were both changing, economically
and culturally. Many attributed the evolution to all the new people moving to Montezuma County, a boom discernable only when
the sun sank behind the Sleeping Ute Mountain. The countryside
looked vacant by day, but the folds of the rolling farm and ranch
land surrendered their secrets by night. Just as Chris and Andrea Jeter noted the increased number of porch lights in McElmo
Canyon, other Montezuma County residents were distressed to
see the night sky lit up by more dwellings. They knew all the new
houses launched the beginning of the end of Montezuma County
as they knew it.

Although the city people flocking to the county didn't typically
create jobs, they generally had more money than locals to help
fuel the local economy. But locals detested the heavier traffic, the
higher real estate prices, and all the new people, except, of
course, when they spent money. Then even Californians, who
shared equal billing with Texans on Cortez's most-hated list of
outsiders, were welcomed, as long as they didn't take up perma-
nent residence. A special disdain was reserved for the burgeon-
ing population of gays and lesbians, considered an affront to all
things American in this Republican, God-fearing, church-going
community.

"They go over like a fart in Sunday school," complained one
businessman, whose opinion expressed the prevailing conviction

of many Cortezians. Change bothered a good number of longtime Montezuma County residents, many of whom would have erected barricades on the highways leading into town, if only it was possible.

The Burnses felt the chilly welcome of a town long closed to outsiders, and they were definitely outsiders. Worse, they were Californians.

"We used to call up friends in LA and ask them over to watch the Lakers," John told me one evening after dinner while we sat in the living room of the family home. "That doesn't happen here. There is something about life here. It is tough to make friends. A lot of people have the cowboy mentality," which is to say Cortezians and Montezumans were extraordinarily independent. If he had called neighbors to come watch the Denver Broncos, he might have had better luck, he realized later. And there was another element to life in a small town.

"You have to be careful about what you say about someone because everyone's related," John told me. "I've put my foot in my mouth."

Offending the locals was just the beginning of a steep learning curve for John and Brenda, who found themselves in terrain so unfamiliar that on one of their first nights in Cortez, they thought they heard the unmistakable rat-a-tat-tat of gunfire. They all hit the floor. John quickly called the police.

The dispatcher, muffling laughter, told John the noise he heard was firecrackers.

"What do you expect?" he asked me, still sounding slightly annoyed at the response. "We lived in LA."

As we compared notes and traded stories, it dawned on me that our arduous transitions to rural America didn't begin to resemble *The Good Life,* a thirty-minute show aired on the Home & Garden cable channel. The show featured urban people moving

to small towns after giving up, or losing through corporate con-
solidations and resulting layoffs, high-powered urban careers.
One episode featured a Wisconsin lawyer who had successfully
argued a case before the U.S. Supreme Court, and he told the
cameras that, despite his professional success, he increasingly
had found his life wanting. He resigned from the bar and opened
a mustard museum in a small Wisconsin town, acknowledging
that his decision shocked family and friends. But the show rarely
showed the gritty side of rural life, and maybe that's because
many of the people featured were wealthy, or at least appeared
to have some money. Neither I nor the Burnses fit the model of
The Good Life, though we were both part of the massive urban
migration the television show reported on weekly.

In time, the Burnses got a stronger hold on life that began with
the purchase of the home in which they now lived. When the
Burnses arrived to see it for the first time, they fell in love with it
right away. There was one renovation they quickly made. They
removed the wood-burning stove that sat along a wall in the
combination living and dining room.

"We had central heat again!" said Brenda. "We're not doing
the lumberjack thing again. I was so happy."

I wasn't so fortunate. The third house I leased, by far the most
comfortable, was still only heated by propane. The large propane
tank that sat a few yards from my house did an adequate job of
keeping the water hot. But it didn't fuel the indoor furnace very
well; the house was always cold or chilly. That was fine on hot
summer days since the place didn't have air conditioning, but
during the winter, I felt as if I was living in a seven-room refrigerator. There was also the added detail of keeping the tank full. I
monitored the gauge frequently, and when the needle began dip-
ping to the red zone, I promptly called a butane supplier, which
sent a large truck to replenish my supply. In two weeks, I went
through an entire tank. At $60 or so a tank, I was going to bank-
rupt myself in my campaign to stay warm.

To stretch my precious fuel, I began using the wood-burning stove. Building a fire, I quickly discovered, was tricky. Once I forgot to open the damper and the kitchen quickly filled with smoke. I had been sitting in my living room when I saw smoke billowing out of the stove. I ran into the kitchen and frantically attempted to open the windows; one was nailed shut, the other painted stuck. No one had ever explained to me the concept of kindling. Instead, I simply stuffed the stove with large logs I gleaned from a large woodpile near my house that my landlord had created from tree trunks and branch cuttings. I finally learned how to start a fire but never quite mastered the art of keeping it going for hours. And I belatedly remembered the advice John and Brenda imparted: keep the woodbin full.

One night, as I reached for a small log, I realized it was my last. I quickly put on my coat and gloves and went outside in the dark, quite unhappy to feel a light drizzle. I marshaled on, collecting soggy pieces of limbs and small logs near the woodpile, hoping I wouldn't meet the raccoon family I had seen foraging for food the week before. Later that night, without enough dry wood to build a fire and too miserly to use my propane, I slept in a thick wool sweater and long underwear with blue jeans. This was high desert country, and the temperatures often plummeted at night even in the summer. The next morning, I went to Wal-Mart to search for relief. The store had stocked three shelves and nearly half an aisle with an assortment of portable space heaters.

"This one is so powerful, it could heat China," said a salesman.

"I just want to heat my house," I replied.

We looked at the various models before settling on the $50 "Heat Buster." The tiny electric space heater became my constant companion as I took it from room to room. When I saw Brenda at Battle Rock one day, I shared details about my search for warmth. We laughed at our transitions to life in rural America. What else could we do?

Chapter 5

Coming Home

Stephen had carefully scheduled several field trips throughout the fall term, and they came just as the children began getting restless. The deft scheduling was the work of an experienced teacher, someone who knew when students needed a break and when, perhaps, he also needed one. In McElmo Canyon the field trips also served another purpose. Although the Internet had shrunk the world and the school's computers allowed the children to visit places far beyond their rural homes, there was still no substitute for seeing the world with your own eyes. Because of Battle Rock's remote location and its distance from cities, the first field trip of the school year took us out of state.

I looked forward to the excursion myself and then wondered why a day in Farmington, New Mexico, was any reason to get excited. And then it occurred to me: since arriving two months earlier, I hadn't been out of town, except for long Sunday drives across the desolate Utah desert. Those sixty days marked the longest stretch in nearly two decades in which I had not lived in or near a major metropolitan area. I had been so busy settling into my new home that I hadn't considered the town's remoteness since arriving—not until I was reminded by the field trip and, as it happened, a poster at a local service station.

As I waited one afternoon at the Texaco Amigo Mart for routine maintenance to be completed on my Jeep, I noticed a narrow poster on the wall listing the distances from Cortez to major American cities. I searched for the closest large cities in the region: 371 miles to Denver, 251 miles to Albuquerque, 403 miles to Phoenix, 347 miles to Salt Lake City. Salt Lake won the prize for the shortest driving time at five hours because there weren't mountains to navigate. But there was another issue. "You don't want to go to Salt Lake in the summer," one of the mechanics said when I asked about the closest cities. "It's hell to drive there in the summer."

Phoenix, he said, was not to be considered at any time. "Too big," he said. Albuquerque took five and a half hours, the poster said. Denver took eight long hours. The distances in the West were immense, but as a son of the region, Stephen wasn't bothered. If he felt the children needed to see a museum, a play, a zoo, he scheduled the trip, planning a semester ahead to take advantage of early bird discounts. In the days leading up to the field trip, the children's excitement rose perceptibly. And, secretly, so did mine.

On the appointed morning, one so foggy that visibility was less than a mile, I arrived at the designated meeting place, the Mobil Corporation field office, and boarded the Montezuma-Cortez School District's flat-nosed activity bus. The bus was luxurious compared with the district's regular buses; it had thick cushioned seats and an overhead rack to store items. One by one, the children arrived. Many of them still looked sleepy.

At 8 A.M. we began our 150-mile round trip to New Mexico, turning onto Highway 160, which led out of Cortez, and past alfalfa fields ready for harvest. The farmhouses and barns were no more than vague shadows in the thick fog. Many of the children slept as the bus followed the dips and swells of the undulating two-lane highway. Tim was curled up in the cushioned seat, only the top of his short-cropped blond hair visible; the third grader's tiny frame was covered by a warm but ill-fitting white jacket. Tim was so quiet that Teresa peeked over the back of her seat to see if he was okay. He was sound asleep.

Sixth graders Harold and Hoshi read a Play Station magazine. Kayla looked out the window, and behind her sat Staton, Tim's little brother. Staton's high-pitched voice could be heard several seats away over the din of the bus. Stephen sat at the rear of the bus, and Teresa had positioned herself three seats behind the bus driver—strategic seating that allowed the two adults to easily monitor everyone between them. I sat across the aisle from Teresa and settled in for the hour-long drive that took us through the Ute Mountain Ute and Navajo reservations and finally into Farmington.

"Look, Cassie, there's Shiprock," said Teresa, pointing at the extraordinary rock formation that sat on the outskirts of one of the Navajo reservation's major communities. "You know, the Navajos consider the mountain sacred," Teresa confided to the children who weren't dozing. "That's why they don't want anyone climbing it."

"When I was a little girl," she went on, "the Navajos used to say that if someone slept on the top, the mountain would move during the night."

The children's eyes were wide now as they peered at the rocky mass. Even in the thick mist, the mountain's dramatic silhouette was clearly visible some thirty miles away. The remnants of a volcano, Shiprock rose sharply from the desert floor, resembling a great schooner with a multitude of masts.

"The mountain would take the person to the other side of life and leave them there." She paused as if imparting a secret. "Then it would return to earth, without them."

Silent, the children peered out at the giant hulk beached along the foggy horizon. The bus rocked on toward Farmington as some of their classmates slept, unaware of Teresa's story and the mystery surrounding a familiar landscape.

Stephen considered himself fortunate to have a classroom aide like Teresa. She was his extra set of hands, eyes, and ears. She wrote the *Battle Rock Bulletin*, the school's two-page, all-color newsletter, and she was the president of the school's Accountability Committee, Battle Rock's version of the Parent Teacher Association. She started the school year as Stephen's unpaid twice-a-week volunteer aide, but he later put her on the payroll for $60 a day.

"You don't have to pay me to do something I love doing," she told him. The teacher won, and paid her for two days' work per week, though she was at the school far more often, even appearing on weekends.

Earlier in the school year, she had organized a cleanup of the Sticker Patch, overtaken by a summer's growth of weeds and painful goat-head thorns. Over the years, tearful children came into the school for first aid after falling or stepping into them. Many soccer balls were flattened. They had to go, Teresa declared one fall day.

Under a sun that quickly turned hot on a Saturday morning, we used hoes to dislodge the stubborn weeds, whose roots sank deep into the ground. Breaking soil that had the strength of concrete was not easy. Stephen and Susan Hanson were banging away at the hard ground, and so were Bill, Teresa's husband, and Kay, Teresa's mother. By early afternoon, the weeds were stacked eight feet tall and then burned, the blaze producing a column of white smoke that rose in the air and fanned into the bright blue sky.

Teresa broke a good sweat that day as she dug at the stubborn clumps of weeds. Even with perspiration at her temples, she retained the wholesome look that had landed her modeling jobs as a teenager. She appeared twice on the pages of *Teen Beat* magazine, modeling blue jeans, blouses, all the latest fashion worn by teenagers in the early 1980s. At thirty-four, she was a pretty woman, her long, honey-blond hair reaching to the middle of her back. When she laughed, it began deep inside and rolled out like waves.

The activity bus rolled into Farmington, and I took in the bustle of the small New Mexico city, its malls, shops, restaurants, and traffic. I made a mental note that if I ever hankered for urban life, I could treat myself to the charms of Farmington and what appeared to be a nice selection of restaurants.

We finally arrived in the parking lot of San Juan College, amid a sea of other yellow buses representing schools from across the Four Corners region. Their teachers had evidently had the same idea as Stephen. Teresa helped line up the children and then made sure those likely to talk to each other during the performance were separated. In the clatter of more than a hundred children, Battle Rock's children settled into the big cushioned seats of the college's theater and became engrossed with a performance of C. S. Lewis's *The Lion, the Witch, and the Wardrobe.*

The students hissed when the witch appeared, applauded the child actors in the play, and gave the cast a thunderous ovation when the play was over. After we ate our brown bag lunches in a Farmington public park, the children boarded the bus, and the driver took a back route to Cortez, traversing dirt roads and narrow bridges. We drove past a herd of buffalo that so enthralled the children that the bus driver stopped for a few minutes so we could see the grazing bison. At about three o'clock, as parents gathered at the Mobil field office, the bus rolled back into Cortez, past industrial warehouses, and past several trailer parks, one of which Teresa Blakney called home.

Cortez was a town with many mobile home parks, with inviting names like *Happy Valley, Orchard,* and *Vista Verde Village.* Some of the communities were folded into the town's tree-lined streets, but most were found at the fringes of the city and beyond, anchored between and behind warehouses and small shops. After a fitful housing search, Bill and Teresa bought their trailer in a nameless park at the western edge of town, not far from the road that led to McElmo Canyon.

For a time—it now seemed an eternity to Teresa—the Blakneys had been solidly middle class, pursuing the trappings through a series of moves that took them several times to Phoenix. On their third and final move to the city, they dug in and began their rocky ascent to prosperity. But urban life, gritty and loud, ultimately drove them back to a smaller and, Teresa thought, more manageable place. Which explained, in part, why they were in Cortez. Teresa's hometown drove her to distraction, but it was still better than living in a city where they had lost more than their middle-class lives.

In the beginning, Phoenix promised a good life, Teresa told me. We sat at a picnic table at the edge of the Sticker Patch eating our lunches while she watched the children playing a soccer match. And in our conversation that day, a few weeks after our trip to Farmington, she calmly described a lifestyle that, in her words, "knocked the wind out of us."

She managed a doctor's office, and Bill launched a home business that provided mediation services for people in debt dealing with their creditors. Both made good money, allowing them to buy a three-bedroom, two-bath home with designer landscaping in a new subdivision outside Phoenix. But the Blakneys seemed to chase the American dream more often than live it, and the pursuit tired Teresa.

"You can get eaten alive in a city," she said told me that day. "When we went back to Phoenix the third time, I couldn't believe it. It would take me an hour and fifteen minutes to drive twelve miles to work. On the news, they would say, 'Don't go outside today, the air's not good.' I was working all the time, and I never got to see Bill, and I never got to see my daughter."

As Bill's business prospered, Teresa quit her job to spend more time with their daughter and help Bill. The timing couldn't have been worse. The Blakneys' business faltered. In these grim stretches, a time in which Teresa noticed Bill went gray at the temples in a matter of months, Teresa increasingly thought about returning to Cortez. The business decline was bad enough, but it was her growing disaffection with Cassie's school that ultimately convinced the family to pack its bags for rural Colorado.

"I went in one day to talk to the teacher, and she didn't even know Cassie's name," said Teresa. "When I told her Cassie was bored with school because the work was too easy, the teacher said, 'This is kindergarten.' I said, 'Cassie already knows the alphabet. She can read.'"

Teresa reached for a book and made her daughter read for her teacher, who was stunned at the child's ability. "Why she didn't know is beyond me," said Teresa, rolling her eyes. After that visit, Teresa seriously began thinking about returning to Montezuma County and to schools where, at least, the teachers knew not only their students' names but also the names of entire families, including grandparents, aunts, uncles, and cousins. Rural communities were like that.

When Teresa learned the local school district in Phoenix planned to install metal detectors in elementary schools, "I told Bill, 'That's it. We're going home.' We left on a Saturday at 11 in the morning, and the temperature was already 116 degrees. I said, 'Thank you, Phoenix, and good-bye.'"

Rolling into Cortez that night after an eight-hour drive, Teresa began to cry.

"What's wrong now?" Bill asked.

"We're home!" she said, making out the dark, massive shadow of the Sleeping Ute Mountain.

Coming home, however, was a decidedly mixed experience. Despite national data that showed the rural economy overall was performing at levels not seen in a generation or more, Cortez didn't begin to possess the jobs or the public and private assistance programs to help lift families into the middle class. There were far fewer job-training programs in a rural community compared with a city and no mass transit to help poor families get to jobs. What jobs there were paid scandalously low wages, which made the job of rural public assistance officials all the more difficult. How does a community help luckless citizens when there's little to offer them?

Bill and Teresa knew all this. Bill had grown up in a small Midwestern town and had lived in a small Georgia community. Teresa had her Cortez roots. But the couple was still shocked at the low wages and the high cost of living, despite a warning in a telephone call from Teresa's younger sister in Cortez to "lower your expectations. You're moving to Cortez." Making ends meet in rural America was different than it was in cities, at once better and worse.

Bill ran through a series of minimum-wage jobs and had luck that ran beyond bad. He broke his hand at one job and was let go. He quit another job when a coworker threatened to take a two-by-four to his boss. In the stifling heat of summer, he blew out one of his knees while walking several miles on hot pavement in another job as a "flagger," a person who waves cautionary orange flags to warn motorists of highway construction crews. Teresa worked at Battle Rock for $120 a week and also held down a part-time job at a liquor store not far from where they lived.

Despite all the hours they worked, the family still qualified for a food box distributed by the U.S. Department of Agriculture. The box, distributed every few weeks, contained different items from month to month, but the family could always count on cereal, raisins, and other nonperishable goods to stretch the family budget. In time, Teresa noticed increasing numbers of families, including some from the Battle Rock community, driving to the distribution point at the Montezuma County Fairgrounds, a collection of nondescript tin-roofed barns and a rodeo arena that sat at the eastern edge of town. Teresa simply drove up to the distribution point, displayed a card, and the box of food was thrust through the window of her old Jeep.

She found the experience humiliating, and the food box reminded her how far the family had slipped economically, but she still wondered some weeks what her family would have done without the government food. In these moments she wished Cortez offered more and better-paying jobs. But this was a minimum-wage town. Employers paid $5.15 an hour, and not a penny more. All of which made treating their daughter's arthritis more difficult. The Blakneys had tried for years to have children, and they were elated when their doctor told them Teresa was pregnant with triplets. But only Cassie survived. Teresa was convinced the multiple births had weakened her daughter's system to such an extent that they were forced to see doctors often, and that posed another problem. The Blakneys' lack of health insurance compelled the family to use a Montezuma County program that helped pay expenses for ill children, but when Teresa used the program, she got a sense of how the town worked—or in this instance, how it didn't.

One week after the school trip to Farmington, Teresa took her daughter to Denver, where they visited an array of specialists. Teresa's sister drove them and also loaned Teresa $350 for the four-day trip. When they returned to Cortez, Teresa submitted her receipts to a county employee. A reimbursement check, the employee told her, would be ready in thirty days.

"About a month after the trip, I went to social services to see if they had my check there, and the receipts were still sitting on the woman's desk and in the same place I left them," said Teresa, with a sigh. "She told me, 'Oh, I must have spaced out.' Then she told me to come back the following week, and the check would be ready. So I did. When I got there, the woman told me, 'Well, it will be another week because I have to verify the receipts.' I said to myself, 'Okay, I'll leave now before I kill you.'"

"It's bad enough to have to ask for assistance," she said later, "but to also be treated this way?"

In the end, Teresa was only reimbursed for a fraction of her travel expenses, far less than the 90 percent reimbursement that she was told she would receive. "Every time I go out to do something in this town, I come back with a story like this."

"That's the way things are in Cortez," said Bill, a soft-spoken man, shaking his head at the incompetence that seemed to run through the fiber of the town. Locals could tell plenty of stories, and they did, about the town's maddening inefficiencies and poor services. Stories about the shoddiness cut across state and local, public and private, office and agency lines. The same was true of cities, of course, but smaller places were supposed to run better. But that was, Teresa discovered, a myth. Poor service was one of Cortez's enduring characteristics, and the uneven attention to details aggravated people trying to make their way with little.

Even more hurtful to Teresa were the urban middle-class and rich Cortezians who, more often than not, looked past, or through, families like the Blakneys as if they didn't exist. Their attitudes bothered Teresa. That Bill held a bachelor's degree in business and that Teresa was halfway to completing her undergraduate degree mattered not to most employers in town, or so it seemed to Teresa. Cortez had a strong anti-intellectual streak buried just below the surface. Many long-timers disdained college-educated people; in a farm and ranch community, education wasn't particularly valued. Urban expatriates noticed the quiet antagonism right away, and in time, so did Bill and Teresa. Bill's difficulty in finding and keeping work—when it came to employment, local ties mattered in Cortez, and Bill Blakney was a Cortezian only by marriage—made Teresa reluctant to finish her degree, despite encouragement from Stephen Hanson. She also worried that the closest four-year college, Fort Lewis College in Durango, would take time better spent with her family. She didn't want to repeat her life in Phoenix, where she never got to see her daughter. And there was the money issue. How to pay for classes? Money always loomed large for the Blakneys, and save for the brush with middle class, Teresa had lived most of her life working to make ends meet, no more, no less. Like the town of Cortez, the Blakneys waited for their ship to dock.

But Teresa still believed that life back home was richer than life in a city, and on many levels easier, because her family was nearby to lend moral support. That was the allure of rural America, the appeal of a small town, at least for Teresa. Life wasn't lived at numbing speed, as it was in Phoenix and in other big cities. Even the schools worked better in a small town, Teresa thought. Cassie, so hesitant and quiet, blossomed at Battle Rock and became more outgoing. Stephen even addressed the issue of her arthritis, which sometimes hobbled the child after an hour of running on the Sticker Patch. On a school hike a year earlier, he had carried Cassie on his back so she could see with the rest of her classmates the Anasazi ruins in nearby Sand Canyon. Teresa knew this wouldn't have happened in Phoenix. But in a small community, there was time to breathe and to really think about what's important, and that had called out to Teresa Blakney in the suburbs of Phoenix. For better or worse, she was home.

Chapter 6

"This Hasn't Been Easy"

*A*s *autumn deepened,* I had a front row seat, literally, to the quickening pace of a harvest. From my vantage point on one of the school's picnic benches during recess or lunch, I watched cattle herds rumble down the road as ranchers on horseback drove their livestock to winter pastures on the canyon's floor. On other days, it was sheep. When I saw neither, the canyon road told me they had been there; it was littered with manure.

When crops and family gardens ripened, I received a cornucopia of produce. Children brought me squash in all colors and shapes, chili and bell peppers, melons, eggplant, and zucchini from family gardens. Others gave me gifts of peach and apricot jams and jellies. Sometimes when I got home, there would be small bags of produce at my door. No note was ever left. Add to this the abundance of apples I received from Mesa and Maya

Lindgren, two tiny blond-haired sisters, and I could have opened my own stand at the local farmers' market.

My treks to the school took me by the Lindgren orchard, one of McElmo's largest. The neat rows of four hundred trees could have been a backdrop for a Norman Rockwell painting, but the artist's work rarely showed the backbreaking effort harvests demanded. I soon experienced how arduous they were.

On a crisp autumn weekend, the sort that transformed Montezuma County into postcard perfection, I joined Eric and Kim and their daughters at their orchard for a weekend of harvesting apples. This will be easy, I thought. But I should have known better. Like finding a house and keeping it warm, there was a challenge to even this seemingly simple task. The Lindgrens gave me a lesson on quickly twisting an apple from the limb without breaking the fragile stem from which the fruit dangled. This was no easy request; the stems were strong and, to my surprise, they had an elastic quality. The slightest amount of pressure applied the wrong way, however, snapped them. Breaking the stem, Kim warned me, meant there would be no apple blossoms on that part of the limb the following spring. Who knew?

There was also a challenge to putting on an apple bib, which had a straitjacket quality. After you put it on, two long ties secured it around your waist. Though the morning was cool, the bib was made of heavy material, and I quickly became hot. On three occasions, I put it on backwards. First Kim, then Eric, then Mesa untangled me.

After my quick lessons, the harvest was on. Eric reached through the branches to pluck the ripened fruit. His torso disappeared into the limbs of the tree, followed by the rustling of leaves and branches. He emerged with several apples protruding from the canvas bib in which we stored them. I followed Eric from tree to tree, some of them so laden with fruit that the boughs scraped the ground. Eric told me to gently lower them in the bag so they wouldn't bruise. He combed the trees quickly, deftly snapping off the apples with a quick twist of his wrist.

Every now and then, we stopped to eat one. The apples were a deep, crimson red that polished to a high gloss when I rubbed them against the bib. And they were sweeter and juicier than any apple I had sampled in years.

Eric was a picking machine, moving efficiently through each tree. For every two trees he combed, I went through one, sampling an apple from just about every tree I visited. I worked the limbs, avoiding the bees and wasps while scratching my hands and arms until they were bleeding. As I plucked the apples, I kept an eye on the knee-high grass around the tree trunks for napping bull snakes and other creatures I had no interest in meeting.

When our apple bags were full, we brought them to Kim. She inspected the fruit on a large sorting table, separating and packing the best ones in boxes. The slightly wormy ones went in another container, destined for applesauce or cider. After a day of picking, my shoulders and back ached from the weight of the apples. How people did this year in, year out, was beyond me.

The organic orchard—no pesticides were used—didn't match last year's harvest of 225 boxes, but the Lindgrens were nonetheless pleased. The trees yielded a crop large enough to fill a seven-box order from an Albuquerque health-food store.

Earlier the Lindgrens told me they had discovered McElmo Canyon nearly two decades earlier as college students traveling the West on a summer trip. The canyon's splendor left an impression, as it did for so many other urban people who visited, and they returned later to buy land. Kim and her daughters had finally moved to the canyon two years ago, but Eric remained in Albuquerque, where he worked as an engineer at the Sandia Laboratories. He commuted to the canyon on Thursday nights and returned Monday mornings. Call it an insurance policy. "We wanted to see how this was going to work," he told me later at the trailer home the family was leasing not far from their orchard.

The Lindgrens quickly learned one truth about their new surroundings. The land that looked so pastoral and inviting from a car window could and did sometimes bite. One year, when the whole family still lived in Albuquerque, the Lindgrens raced to McElmo Canyon to beat an approaching snowstorm. Eric picked apples in the driving wind and snow until two in the morning, while Kim sorted and boxed the apples in a trailer they had parked nearby.

She sometimes wondered aloud what they were doing in a rural place, living a lifestyle that often required consulting a stack of how-to books that sat on their coffee table. The exercise amused her, especially when she consulted a book titled *How to Raise Sheep the Modern Way.*

"The sheep, for instance," said Kim, beginning to recite a list of items they had to learn. This weekend, one of the sheep had broken into a bag of grain and nearly died because it ate too much. Kim forced milk of magnesia for sheep down the animal's throat. She periodically checked on the animal the weekend we picked apples. I noticed that it rested beneath an apple tree in the tall, cool grass. Kim was relieved when it showed signs of stirring.

"For instance, for instance, for instance, for instance, for instance," said Eric with a smile that masked a weariness. "We haven't figured out pears yet." Indeed, I looked at the rows of pear trees standing next to the apple trees. Except to pick them for their own table, the Lindgrens did not bother with them this year. As the family carved out its place in the country, nothing was simple or easy, least of all the issue of water—who got it and when.

The Black Dike Ditch meandered at the edge of the Lindgren orchard. Named for a ridge of volcanic rock that sat atop a hill and resembled the folds of an accordion, the Black Dike Ditch was roughly four miles long and served nine families. Aside from its unusual name, the Black Dike Ditch was distinct in another way. Most of the Black Dike's water users were urban expatriates who didn't know the ins and outs of water law that many rural families possessed. As a result, the Black Dike Ditch Committee struggled mightily to produce bylaws that governed use of the ditch that snaked along the canyon floor.

Eric arrived with an agenda for a meeting one Sunday afternoon, and so did another property owner, Penny Southworth. The agendas didn't resemble each other, but that was the least of the problems. People were in a foul humor over the unsuccessful months-long effort to produce bylaws for the ditch's water users. I sat next to Eric and watched a beautiful autumn afternoon turn stormy.

People talked over each other. Sometimes three people talked at the same time. Twice Penny was interrupted. She put her foot down. "You keep interrupting me," she said with exasperation looking at Eric.

Self-governance looked good on paper, but it could be a headache. And though there were advantages to rural life, I decided that serving on a ditch committee was not one of them. The meetings consumed too much time, and there were all those flowcharts that Bill Southworth, Penny's husband, used to manage the meeting. Kim had approached the Southworths to tell them the meetings had to change. Some of Penny's unhappiness evidently stemmed from the fact that she felt unappreciated, a ditch member whispered to me later.

"Someone else can take the minutes," she snapped, as the meeting progressed.

But the Black Dike Ditch Committee also didn't have a president or vice president. For the first hour of what became a four-hour meeting, there wasn't much order. There were other issues that confronted the ditch committee, including how to monitor the earthen canal to make sure it didn't collapse. Ditches that caved in on themselves were bad business indeed, and collapsing ditches occurred periodically, mostly because of neglect. Eric suggested a "ditch boss" who would walk the canal daily. People balked. Though everyone was fit in these rural parts, walking four miles a day beside a ditch was still four miles a day. Once a week was often enough, ditch members decided.

About this time, I concluded there was still at least one good reason for maintaining an urban address. When I turned on the faucet, I was reasonably assured water flowed into my sink or out of my sprinkler. I didn't have to worry about maintaining the water main. That was someone else's concern. The ditch water wasn't potable, but it was every bit as important as drinking water. Ditches supplied water for fields, gardens, and livestock. You had to pay attention to water flow, clean the ditches, and keep the earthen walls strong.

Eric amazed me. I concluded that the Lindgrens, and other city people who willingly moved to rural America, were definitely urban people cut from a different kind of cloth. I thought of friends in New York, Washington, D.C., San Francisco, and Dallas. Not one of them would have survived this place; most of them wouldn't have even tried. Not that they weren't resilient. But rural living demanded attention to detail on such a minute level, and no one I knew would have been interested in dealing with ditches, fending off wildlife, tending orchards, picking apples in a storm in the middle of a night. Living life with the volume turned down, as one Los Angeles friend called a quieter lifestyle, appealed to many of my friends as we settled into our forties and fifties. Some of my friends even harbored dreams of living like the Lindgrens, but they had no idea that life with the volume turned down also included a lot of static that urban ears weren't accustomed to hearing. In the end, a rural life was not quiet or relaxing.

When the meeting adjourned, the tension evaporated. The hostess, Judy Lane, served soft drinks and homemade pie made with apples from her small orchard. As Black Dike Ditch Committee members chatted, the sound of water running through the ditch could be heard at the edge of the Lanes' backyard. Without the water, there would be no plants in the rock garden, no apples from the orchard to make pies, and no grapes from the vines that grew throughout the property. Water was a valuable commodity in McElmo Canyon, so it was no surprise that ditch committee members turned cranky during meetings. People were talking about livelihoods that were, in effect, governed by a nineteenth-century Colorado statute, a law that loomed large over the water-starved West, then as now.

More than a century after its enactment, the statute was still largely intact and so well written—at least Colorado water officials thought so—that other western states used the state's water law as a blueprint. In truth, water law was a confusing array of statutes and amendments to anyone who read them for the first time, or even a second time. Largely predicated on the notion of first come, first served, water rights could be, and often were, transferred to subsequent buyers. This wasn't ordinarily a problem, but water rights could also be sold to landowners many miles away from the source, and that's when confusion set in for the uninitiated. The repeated sale of real estate and subsequent transfer of water rights over the decades created such a tangle of paperwork for some property owners that they faced steep learning curves if they wanted water. For all the complexities, the actual consumption was relatively simple, as was its measurement. People tracked their water use through gates set into the ditch. The gates—some of which opened and closed automatically—were equipped with gauges that measured the water flow, and when the correct amount had rushed through the portal, the gate was closed.

Water is so precious that many ditch users—the dishonest ones, at least—stole, or tried to steal, more than their allotment of water. They usually waited until the middle of the night to divert the water by conveniently forgetting to close the gate that regulated the flow. Neighbors downstream awakened to find the ditch's level suspiciously low. This rural-style hijacking, of course, led to fights, as neighbor pummeled neighbor with fists, or drew knives, or sometimes even fired guns.

Old-timers told me about two families who drew their guns on each other during a water hearing in the 1950s at the Montezuma County Courthouse. The story may have been apocryphal, but I heard it so many times and with slightly different twists from old-timers that some of it had to be true, I figured, despite the fact that an exhaustive search of old newspapers at the local library turned up nothing.

"Real Hatfield and McCoy stuff," one grizzled man said after he told me the story. The two families had been warring for years over water, accusing each other of taking more than their share. The dispute finally landed the two families in court, where, in a heated moment, they drew guns and fired on each other. Or so the story went.

These days, water hearings could still be lively proceedings, but they were held in a stately building in downtown Durango, some fifty miles away, and they were, on the whole, far more sedate since lawyers had largely taken them over. But that didn't mean issues over water were any less contentious. Penny Southworth didn't attend the next meeting of the Black Dike Ditch Committee, even though it was held in the elegant, two-story adobe-style home she shared with her husband. She had booked an out-of-town trip. Nothing provoked more discord in McElmo Canyon than water, except perhaps the fights over the direction of Battle Rock school.

On the apple harvest's second day, I was better at snapping the apples without breaking the stems. The trick was in the wrist action. But I would never be as proficient as Eric, who showed no ill effects from hours of picking the day before. Despite a long, hot shower and solid sleep the night before, my back was still stiff. My arms were sore; the constant motion of reaching upward had left them heavy, and I found the second day more demanding.

Eric had brought a ladder to reach the upper boughs of the tree. I gamely climbed up and down the ladder, leaning into the apple trees to pick the fruit. Halfway down the ladder, I felt the sharp pain of an insect sting. I swung around to swat a wasp, lost my balance, and fell off the ladder. In the seconds it took me to fall the four or five feet, I managed to produce a string of profanity that, when I thought about it later, impressed even me. Suddenly, I found myself on my back. My arm and the thick grass had broken my fall. Thankfully, no one was around. Trees obscured me from Eric and Kim, who were at the apple-sorting table. I picked myself up and gingerly wandered back to the table. Kim announced we had picked enough apples to fill the order for the Albuquerque health-food store. Before I drove home, the Lindgrens gave me two small bags of apples. The apples lasted two weeks, roughly the period of time it took for the last of the scratches on my arms to heal.

As the couple maintained a commuter marriage through a second year, Kim plunged headfirst into carving rural lives for her and her daughters, Mesa and Maya. That included the acquisition of several sheep, a variety of chickens, and Lucky, a near-toothless stray that wandered one Sunday afternoon to the Lindgrens' trailer home. Add to those animals a light-brown burro named Ruby, and Kim could have opened a petting zoo.

Ruby was no ordinary burro. The donkey had papers, compliments of the Bureau of Land Management. The BLM in the 1980s rescued burros and wild horses from the canyons and mountains situated on public lands in the West and then put the animals up for adoption. Ruby was one of the burros retrieved in the widely publicized wild animal rescues, and rural families in the West flocked to adopt the animals. Ruby first found herself with an owner in Socorro, New Mexico, then with the Lindgrens in McElmo Canyon after Kim learned about the burro airlift and found out that Ruby was available. Like the urban people who took the oddest of paths to Montezuma County, so did some of the animals that called McElmo Canyon home.

When the girls weren't riding or feeding their burro, they sometimes explored the century-old cemetery located at the foot of the canyon wall. The cemetery marked the final resting places of the Mormon settlers who had tamed this wild land at the end of the nineteenth century. The education the girls received in their new home was rich and included the Battle Rock 4-H Club, headed for more than four decades by Audrey Allmon. After her retirement from Battle Rock, Audrey poured even more energy into one of Montezuma County's most decorated youth organizations. But Kim found the transition to rural life taxing.

"This hasn't been easy," Kim admitted to me one day while I was visiting. "When we were in Albuquerque and a friend was helping me get our house ready for sale, another friend came by and asked, 'Why are you doing this? You had a good thing here.' We did have a good life in Albuquerque, but all I know is that, by the time we left, it was over."

Not everything in McElmo Canyon posed uphill battles for the Lindgrens. At the far end of the apple orchard, Kim's vegetable and flower garden flourished, a triumph she enjoyed early on.

"Old-timers say you plant when the snow is completely off the Sleeping Ute, and that's good enough for me," she said, as we walked through her garden, inspecting the varieties of tomatoes, squash, corn, and melons.

At Battle Rock one day, Mesa and Maya snacked on multicolored corn as the rest of the children gathered with wide eyes around the sisters over the unusual snack. On other occasions, Kim sent Stephen bags of vegetables, tomatoes, squash, cucumber—whatever had ripened that week. Some of the vegetables and fruit came from so-called heritage seeds, produce that was no longer grown in quantity because it didn't possess a long shelf life; over the decades, agribusiness had bred vegetables and fruit to a hardiness to survive the transport to urban markets. Kim rolled back the years in her garden, as elsewhere on the Lindgren orchard, but other details of rural life proved more challenging. One night she showed up at a Battle Rock school board meeting, held in the one-room school, and shortly after she sat down, an aroma began drifting through the room.

"What is that smell?" one board member asked, crinkling her nose. "Does anyone smell anything?"

I did notice a foul odor in the air, and checked the bottom of my shoes. Others did the same, and the source was quickly found. Hanging from the bottom of one of Kim's shoes was a large clump of sheep manure.

"Oh, my!" she exclaimed with a startled smile. She left and returned with clean shoes, and received friendly nods and smiles from the other board members. Many of them, like Kim, were urban transplants, and they had been there, too, with sheep, cow, and horse manure stuck to the bottoms of their shoes. For all the demands of country living, the Lindgrens lived abundant lives, made richer—at least in the beginning, Kim thought—by the one-room school down the road.

But when she won election to the Battle Rock school board, she saw aspects of the school that made her uneasy. The reliance on computer software to gauge student progress bothered her. Stephen heard her concerns and hired another part-time teacher, Anne Wright, to teach math and science. In time, Kim saw what she considered other deficiencies. The curriculum could be stronger, she thought. But she let her concerns sit for the fall term. She studied the school and the canyon because she didn't want to be "one of those city people who came in and thought she knew everything," as she put it one day. When she finally pursued those issues in the spring, there were unhappy consequences for her, Stephen, and the canyon community.

Chapter 7

The Boat Races

*A*nne Wright raised her voice above the cantankerous first graders, impatient for recess. She asked for their attention, which didn't come quickly. The noise didn't ebb until Stephen bellowed in his teacher's voice from the back of the room, "Quiet!"

Anne gave Stephen a thankful look, and she introduced herself. She was the new math and science teacher, and this was her first day at the school.

"What do you want to study this year?" Anne asked the class.

"Dinosaurs!" yelled one child.

"Outer space!" said another.

"Aliens!" said Staton.

Anne stopped. "That might be tricky," she said to the class, without breaking a hint of a smile.

"I want to dissect!" cried out another student.

"I want to study brains!" said another child.

"We can make brain Jell-O and eat it," Anne said, this time smiling.

"Ee-ee-eu-oo-ooh!" cried the class.

Stephen, who had been working at the back of the school setting up a new copy machine, looked at Anne with a smile. Teresa chuckled. At the end of Anne's introduction, an older girl got up from her chair in her high-heel tennis shoes and gave Anne a hug.

"Thank you," the girl said.

"Thank you," Anne replied.

After lunch, Anne launched the class on its first science lesson. "What is science?" she asked the students.

"Oh, please, I know, I know!" said a first grader, raising her hand enthusiastically.

Anne called on her. The girl twisted her face.

"Um, um, I forgot."

A third grader helped her younger classmate: "Learning about things we don't know."

"Yeah, that's it," the first grader said.

Anne paused, then proceeded, deciding the response was a good start. "Okay, who is a scientist?"

"A person who studies science," Kayla said.

Anne hesitated again, then proceeded, deciding that this answer too was good enough to launch the class into conducting a very simple experiment.

"Science is the study of living and nonliving organisms, and you are all scientists!" she told the class. They smiled.

She took them through the scientific method—asking a question, making a guess, conducting research—and then dispatched the students at each table on a project that involved soda water, carbonated soda, and raisins. Some of the younger children tried to eat the raisins, but Anne put a stop to that.

"What do you think raisins will do in water?" she asked the class.

"Float!"

"Sink!"

"Explode!"

"Expand!"

"Shrink!"

The answers came all at once from the four corners of the room.

"How do you spell *float*?" asked a first grader.

In a multi-age classroom, spelling sometimes blurred with science. One of the older children spelled F-L-O-A-T for the first grader, and then Anne put small clear plastic cups on each table, poured soda water into the cups and dropped three raisins in each. The raisins wiggled and fell sideways; some floated to the top of the cup and then fell back to the bottom. Others collected massive amounts of bubbles and quivered in the fluid. Others turned over and over. Every move of the raisins brought exclamations of "Wow!" "Neat!" and "Look at that!"

The class wrote down the results and added an illustration. "The only wrong conclusion is no conclusion," Anne yelled above the students, who were still watching the raisins do acrobatics in the carbonated soda.

"The raisins are lighter than the water," Kayla said.

"Yes!" said Anne.

*A*nne *had never before taught* in a one-room school, and the experience was an education. "We all learned some things today!" she told Stephen at the end of her first day.

Stephen had hired Anne after considering Kim's concerns about the school's curriculum. Her presence—and more to the point, her salary—was paid by a $300,000 grant Battle Rock and five other Colorado rural schools had received three years earlier from the Annenberg Foundation. Battle Rock's share in each of the three years was $20,000, and Stephen used it liberally. The Annenberg money paid for Battle Rock's numerous field trips, from Farmington to Durango. The money also paid for a wealth of computer software that supplemented grammar, reading, math, and science lessons, and it paid for some of the computers.

The St. Davids, Pennsylvania, foundation, through its Annenberg Rural Challenge, dispensed $50 million to seven hundred schools in thirty-five states in the 1990s. From New England, to the Deep South, to the West, to Alaska and Hawaii, these tiny schools and their communities benefited in ways large and small from the money made possible by Walter H. Annenberg, a former U.S. Ambassador to the Court of St. James. Some schools started their community's only newspaper. Others studied endangered wetlands. Some recorded the oral histories of their community's oldest residents.

The Rural Challenge was the latest in a long tradition of Annenberg support for educational interests of every kind. The Corporation for Public Broadcasting and the University of Southern California and the University of Pennsylvania, where schools of communication bear Annenberg's name, received generous endowments and subsequent gifts. The former ambassador also awarded $500 million to the nation's public schools in 1994 in a White House ceremony; it remains the single largest gift ever given to public education. A year later, the foundation created the most ambitious program of its kind with the Rural Challenge, designed to not only improve rural schools but also rebuild their communities.

No one remotely suggested that the Annenberg Rural Challenge alone in a handful of years could correct the long and steady deterioration of rural America and its schools. Nor did anyone suggest that aggressive makeovers were possible for all rural schools and their communities. The proposition was simply too expensive. But communities like McElmo Canyon and schools like Battle Rock that received money were given an unprecedented opportunity to transform themselves. "Without the Annenberg money, Battle Rock would be just another rural school," Stephen told me one day at school. "It's transformed the school."

The Annenberg program also helped remake rural teachers. The foundation and others lent support to an inventive master's degree program for rural teachers headquartered at Middlebury College's Bread Loaf School of English. Stephen was among the teachers accepted by the Vermont college, and he received stipends from the Rural Challenge and the DeWitt Wallace–Reader's Digest Fund to attend summer classes taught by the country's best liberal arts professors. At the end of five summers, Stephen and his peers earned master's degrees from Middlebury, which hosted the summer courses along with Oxford University and St. John's College near Santa Fe.

The quiet rebirth of rural schools didn't go unnoticed. The flagging achievement of urban children prompted some city school systems to try to create what Battle Rock and other schools like it represented: small classes where older children assisted younger classmates and where students were grouped by ability rather than by grade level. Some city school districts tried to create smaller schools within large school buildings by dedicating wings of a building to a single grade. Other urban districts removed some of the boundaries of grades, grouping students in first through third grades in the same classroom. Research showed that stability in the early grades was critical, and in the 1990s many schools embraced the notion by allowing teachers to "travel" with their students through the primary grades. This was the more personal approach Battle Rock had always held to. But the approach also created more work for teachers.

In her early weeks at Battle Rock, Anne discovered what others who taught in one-room schools had long known: a multi-age classroom was a far more difficult assignment than a single-grade classroom. She worked around the challenge by sometimes giving everyone the same assignment, instructing the younger children to work only to a certain point. Sometimes, they all worked the same assignment, with the older kids assisting their younger classmates.

Stephen gave Anne free rein, and with this rare gift of workplace freedom, she transformed math and science into inviting lessons, blending the two subjects and the outdoors in Battle Rock's time-honored approach to schooling. One fall afternoon, she staged a boat race in the Rock Ridge Ditch, which ran next to Battle Rock. She teamed older kids with the younger children, and each team calculated the speed at which the water flowed in the ditch. They measured the distance from a cottonwood tree that sprouted from the bank to a point fifty-six feet downstream. The students dropped an empty film canister into the murky water, and using a stopwatch, they timed how quickly the canister traveled the distance. The children repeated the exercise two more times.

"Why are we doing this?" Anne asked them, yelling over the noise of the rushing water and the clapping of the broad cottonwood leaves.

"To get an average!" several students yelled back, their faces pressed against the tall chain-link fence that separated the school from the ditch, observing the first-day-of-school rule that Stephen had imposed. No one was allowed near the ditch unless accompanied by an adult.

They went back into the school and worked the numbers, with the fifth and sixth graders helping the younger kids. Then the fun began. The day before, the children had made boats out of white plastic plates, straws, and plastic containers of all kinds. Using glue, tissue, and magic markers, the children decorated the plastic plates. Some of the creations set shipbuilding back a millennium; others were amazingly sophisticated.

The first boat down the ditch was the H_2O Boat. Four straws glued to the middle of the plate supported a canopy of tissue paper. The crude craft capsized midstream down and was a soggy mess by the time it landed in the fish net placed in the ditch to catch the boats. The boat's designers were disappointed with their time of 25 seconds. Two more boats shaved a second off the time, and then the U.S.S. *Pardy*—it should have been *Party,* but this was math and science, not spelling—took its place upstream.

The boat got caught on roots twice. The children retrieved it, and on the third attempt, the U.S.S. *Pardy* bobbed down the stream before the force of the current pushed it to the slower-moving water near the bank. Its time: an unimpressive 35 seconds.

"Big-time loser!" yelled one student from behind the fence, laughing. The U.S.S. *Pardy*'s no-frills design—it was no more than the plastic plate Anne had given the children—was meant to give it speed. Tim scratched at his blond hair over his boat's miserable time.

Kayla and her younger classmate were the final competitors. The Shade Boat, boasting a multicolored sail of red, orange, yellow, and blue, attacked the current and then completely flipped over. The colorful sail disappeared into the brown water. Somehow—call it a maritime miracle—the boat slipped into the fish net upside down, barely discernable in the murky water, at 20.6 seconds.

"We won!" yelled a surprised Kayla, as her second-grade classmate jumped up and down in delight.

Anne eventually spearheaded lessons that took students on an exploration of Montezuma County. The classes were a living textbook that celebrated the region's history, environment, wildlife, and the local economy. The treks into the county's nooks and crannies, to the Cortez livestock auction barn, to the Anasazi ruins that speckled the countryside, also illustrated one irrefutable fact: Montezuma County was changing more and more every year. The sprawling county was still very much rural, but every year it lost a bit of its country ambiance. The fields that once yielded alfalfa or beans or provided pasture for cattle and sheep now produced a harvest of another kind, new, custom-built homes and expansive subdivisions.

Chapter 8

The Cloakroom

On a morning too inviting to spend indoors, Tumiko Murphy led the school's youngest children on a hike along the base of the canyon wall. I followed Tim, Staton, and several other children on the crisp autumn morning until the school disappeared behind the swells of the rolling terrain. After we walked for fifteen minutes, she stopped at a small clearing surrounded on three sides by trees and waited for the children to settle before beginning her Spanish lesson.

Battle Rock was a family affair for Tumiko. Her son, Hoshi, was a sixth grader at the school, and her husband, Paul, sat on the Battle Rock school board. In rural schools, whole families were involved in the education of children. Tumiko came to the school every week and, weather permitting, convened her classes outdoors. The outdoor classes were one of the remaining traditions that survived the school's tumultuous updating. But the outdoors posed challenges for Stephen's stable of part-time teachers, which included parents like Tumiko. For the canyon that provided seemingly endless opportunities for lessons of every kind also generated just as many distractions. When the children were reasonably quiet, she began the class that ultimately became a lesson for her.

"Let's practice the days of the week," she said, sitting on a small boulder beneath a cedar tree.

"Dominguez, Lunes, Martes," the children said unevenly, following her lead. Staton's high-pitched voice could be heard above the rest of the children. "Miércoles, Jueves, Viernes, and Sabado."

"Excellent!" Tumiko said, as bits of tree bark fell on her head.

First graders, unbeknownst to her, had climbed a cedar tree behind her sometime between Dominguez and Sabado and begun stripping bark and tips of the rough cedar leaves. Most of the bark seemed to fall in Tumiko's hair and on the back of her sweater. By the time she noticed the children in the tree, the back of her sweater, I noticed, was covered in pieces of bark.

"You boys and girls get down now," she said, looking up, shielding her eyes as the rain of bark and leaves continued. The children paid her no mind, and Tumiko returned to the lesson, ignoring them.

"Okay, does anyone remember the numbers in Spanish?" she asked, the back of her sweater and head almost completely covered now by the soft bark of the cedar.

"Uno, dos, tres," the children chanted, as others began playing with the dirt and rocks behind Tumiko, erecting a small version of the Anasazi ruins at Mesa Verde National Park. She noticed the children playing in the dirt and chastised them.

"What are you children doing?" she asked. "Get out of the dirt."

They also didn't heed her. Tumiko was a soft-spoken woman with a gentle demeanor. But in the next breath, she summoned Stephen's name.

"I don't want to tell Mr. Hanson that you were not good children," she said.

Her tone was not in the least bit menacing. All she needed to do was invoke the name of Stephen. They stopped stripping the bark off the cedar, and construction halted on the miniature earthen city. Subsequent meetings with the children went much better, when she learned to effectively summon the name of Stephen Hanson, who, as the children well knew, didn't brook foolishness.

Stephen ran Battle Rock with a kind of tough love dispensed in the school's cloakroom. By the middle of the fall, about a third of the children had been summoned to the tiny room for summits with Stephen for a range of infractions that included arguing with or hitting a classmate, talking excessively, or not doing class work. School discipline had evolved significantly since Battle Rock was built in 1915; no longer was it acceptable for a teacher to paddle a student. Under the threat of lawsuits from parents and a growing number of studies indicating corporal punishment was counterproductive, teachers turned to other alternatives. In Stephen's case, the tiny cloakroom served as the place where he dispensed the school's brand of punishment. After admonishing students for their misdeeds, he ordered them to sit on the room's long, narrow wooden bench for hours at a time. Built to accommodate the indoor bathrooms that rural families had opposed years earlier, the cloakroom and the bench were heavily trafficked with children who had committed one infraction or another.

One morning, as Stephen watched a student take a reading comprehension test on a computer, trouble began brewing at the back of the room. Second grader Missy, a rambunctious girl with a black pageboy, taunted Harold, who had a penchant for talking with his classmates. The teacher had heard Harold's whispers of "Stop it!" become louder. Stephen turned to see Missy jab Harold, and Harold return the favor.

"You two come here!" he bellowed.

They got up out of their chairs and walked out to the cloak-room with the teacher, who closed the door and sat the two on the long bench. The door was shut for a very long time until it opened quietly and Harold walked back into the classroom. Students who returned from these meetings couldn't buy eye contact with their classmates, who looked down, away, anywhere but at the condemned soul coming back from the cloakroom. Some of the children gave Harold disapproving looks as he walked to his chair.

"I'm glad she got into trouble," Harold hissed at a classmate who wagged a disapproving finger at the boy. He pushed his glasses back up on his nose and sat by himself fuming the rest of the morning. Missy was banished to the bench in the cloakroom, an even bigger outcast than her sixth-grade classmate.

In Stephen's absence, the students had unwisely decided to take a break from their work. The children visited in whispered tones that grew progressively louder. Some of the children had even left their chairs and were talking with classmates at other tables. By the time Stephen returned, conversations and laughter were in full bloom.

"Freeze!" ordered Stephen.

Children stopped in their tracks, and the teacher could see who was doing what. Most of the time when Stephen felt compelled to yell "Freeze!" students typically were not doing their work.

"All of you guys need to have your books open and be reading," said Stephen in a voice that told the class that he was not messing around. "Quietly."

He looked at Hoshi, slow to open his book.

"Do I need to call your mother?" Stephen asked the boy. The book was opened.

"I'm coming around and checking on your reading progress. I hope you have some good news for me!"

Happily for Stephen, they did.

The children kept Stephen alert, and he spent much of his time managing his high-spirited students. They also kept me on my toes. Some of the children turned to me when Stephen and Teresa were busy with other children, and as they became more comfortable with me, I helped them with their math, assisted them with their essays, or helped them select books to read. But I was also pulled into the contentious world of school discipline, a role I most definitely did not relish.

Several days after her altercation with Harold, Missy was reprimanded again and dispatched to the cloakroom bench. I had seen the disagreement unfold between Missy and another child and knew the girl was getting her just reward. A half-time teacher had told Stephen about Missy's aggression, and Stephen had banished the second grader to the bench. When I went to my Jeep to retrieve my lunch, I successfully walked by the girl before she was able to say anything. I wasn't so lucky when I returned. She was waiting.

She stopped me, told me her version of the story, and then dried her tears. "Can I go to my seat now?" she asked.

"You'll have to ask Mr. Hanson," I said, trying to extricate myself. Her mood changed when she realized I could do nothing for her, and then she lambasted the half-time teacher.

"She's the meanest teacher in the whole, wide world!" Missy yelled, as she coaxed another stream of tears.

I ducked into the classroom, and Stephen shot me a weary look as the girl's sobs filtered into the room. He had told me earlier that he worried about Missy and her behavior more than the other students. "She listens to me now, but I feel like I'm losing her," he told me one afternoon.

There were reasons I later discovered that helped explain Missy's behavior. She approached me one afternoon at the third-grade table, where I was reading a book with Tim about pioneers settling the West.

"Bill, I want to show you this."

She thrust an envelope at me. I looked at the return address and realized the letter had been mailed from a Colorado prison. Before I could ask her who had written the letter, she volunteered the author.

"My father wrote me," she said. "You want to read it?"

"Okay," I said, completely surprised at the child's honesty. I left Tim reading his book and went to one of the big blue-cushioned chairs. Both of them were empty, and Missy and I had as much privacy as was possible in a one-room school.

I carefully opened the letter, and Missy watched me intently as I read it. Full of misspellings and grammatical errors, the one-page letter expressed a father's love for his daughter. She didn't get to see her father very often, Stephen later told me when I asked, because he was serving a long sentence for drug trafficking. There was that, and the fact that her mother was recovering from cancer. That was a lot for a second grader to confront.

Stephen worried about the girl, and he spent a lot of time in the cloakroom with Missy and other children. The school day was a minefield of disciplinary cases for Stephen, but an equal amount of the trouble occurred on the Sticker Patch.

One day Tim and Troy, the first-grade boy whose baby sister had died earlier in the fall, locked horns during a heated soccer match. Troy and the younger boys had been beaten all fall, but they had finally come close to toppling their older classmates, including Tim. When Stephen rang the bell ending recess, the children trooped into the school. The competitive juices were still flowing as Troy calmly looked at Tim and then shot his older classmate the middle finger.

"Bring it on," said Tim.

Stephen saw the whole exchange and descended on the boys like an eagle diving for prey. The two boys were hauled out to the cloakroom for another one of the teacher's summits. This time, the teacher imposed bans on recess. Maybe it was all the canyon's fresh air that made them boisterous. But the teacher rode the children in long stretches for misbehaving or not doing their work. After disciplining unruly students in those long talks in the cloakroom, the behavioral problems disappeared for a few days, and there was peace, but only for a few days. Then Stephen was forced to reprimand students again. More often than not, he admonished Harold for not doing his work or Missy for talking too much. Just as often, it seemed, he refereed spats between the two.

They tangled one day when Harold brought his prized glider to school. At the end of the day, while they were waiting in line outside the school for the bus to arrive to take them home, Missy turned and accidentally knocked the tail off the plane. Tears welled up in Harold's eyes, and he would have throttled Missy had Stephen not seen that the adversaries were on the verge of another battle.

"I'll pay you back," a remorseful Missy said.

From personal experience, the teacher knew there would be repercussions. The next day, Stephen asked them what their parents had said. Harold said his father told him Missy should replace the plane. Harold's father actually called the school, telling Stephen, "If someone breaks someone else's toy, then they should replace it." The toy could be replaced, of course, but not by Missy, her mother said. Harold was at fault, she said, for bringing his glider to school.

Stephen shared the story with his wife, Susan, that night as I dined with the couple.

"The lives of children!" she exclaimed, as we laughed.

But even as Stephen found the glider incident humorous, another issue was brewing at the school that a cloakroom conference wasn't going to repair. At a point in the fall, it was difficult to ascertain when, Debbie and Connie, two of the older girls, ostracized Kayla. Kayla, who was the only other girl in the sixth grade, never mentioned the rift to Stephen, at least not immediately. Never one to complain, Kayla simply suffered in silence. The two girls were loud and boisterous and rude to many of their classmates, and Stephen had called them on their behavior. Not that it had any lasting effect. The rift between the girls surprised

Stephen when he learned about it weeks later, and this time the parents became involved.

For the most part, however, Stephen's hard-line approach kept most of his students in their places most of the time, even if they chafed under his discipline. One afternoon, as children finished grammar lessons, one boy began closing his English book when he noticed writing on the last page. The boy showed his class-mates. Some of them giggled. Others covered their mouths in horror. Writing in a book was bad enough, but using a pen was unforgivable. Those sins were compounded by what was actually written. The children decided Missy had written the message be-cause the scrawl resembled her handwriting. When confronted by her classmates, she vigorously shook her head "no" and be-gan crying. The boy finally summoned Stephen to look at the discovery.

The teacher looked at the short note. He showed me the back page of the book, and the corners of his mouth betrayed a slight smile. "Mr. Hanson," the message read, "is stupider than a box of rocks."

Chapter 9

"The Friendliest Town in the West"

McElmo Canyon was the sort of place where cultures past and present blended nearly seamlessly, at least on a collection of boulders that sat near the Utah state line several miles past Battle Rock. The canyon was so immense and so nuanced, it was difficult to see everything in the first, second, or even sixth trip, which is when I actually noticed the shadows in the boulders. I was traveling to Hovenweep National Monument, a haunting collection of Anasazi ruins some fifty miles from Cortez, when I slowed down and then stopped to inspect the monstrous rocks more closely. There, tucked into the red and pink boulders, were Anasazi ruins. I hiked up into the boulders, which had created a natural shelter for the ruins, when I noticed something else even more astonishing: Anasazi carvings were engraved in the rocks. Interspersed around the carvings were cattle brands that had been chiseled into the rock only a century earlier by cowboys passing through the canyon on cattle drives. And mingled with the Anasazi and cattle brand impressions were Navajo engravings of an indeterminate age, next to modern-day messages with names and dates of passersby. "Historical graffiti," one local historian called the collection of markings.

The melding of cultures was celebrated in the Cortez Cultural Center, a two-story museum and arts center, and the region's embrace of its multicultural history was important to people like Tumiko for reasons that were readily apparent when I saw her again at Battle Rock. When she arrived for her weekly Spanish lessons, she wore a Japanese-style straw hat. Her colorful ankle-length skirt featured a vaguely Latin American pattern, and she was wrapped in a plaid hunter's jacket, the local uniform on brisk days.

Ever since I met Tumiko earlier in the school year, she had intrigued me. I wondered how someone born in Tokyo who attended college in Mexico City and then lived in Los Angeles had found herself in a place like McElmo Canyon. Like the etchings on the rocks, Tumiko managed her blended heritage with a calm silence. Negotiating attitudes in the West's friendliest town was another matter altogether.

Cortez actually billed itself as "The Friendliest Town in the West" on a small marquee that was so oddly placed at the edge of downtown that it took me months to realize it was even there. Out of motorists' line of vision, the sign sat on a small island of grass and was the sort of marquee that many small communities typically construct near the town square or near city hall and where local civic clubs announce pancake breakfasts or spaghetti dinners. But there was never a message on the marquee, except for the town's moniker.

The sign was an inside joke among some new residents from cities who could have made a strong argument against the claim. Could a town, they wondered, be sued for false advertising? Tumiko might have wondered the same thing, but she was too earnest, too gracious, to make the snide remarks, even after she confronted her new home's dark side.

"I had a hard time adjusting, and I'm still adjusting," she told me as we walked back to the school along the canyon wall after that week's Spanish lesson. "But this is a peaceful place, and it's a good place to raise children." Before she left, I received an invitation for dinner that night.

When I arrived, Tumiko was dicing vegetables for chicken soup. She had killed a hen earlier that day, a detail I was happy to have missed. As she prepared dinner, I sat at the kitchen table and listened to how she found herself in Montezuma County.

Her mother was an El Salvadoran freedom fighter; her father, a married Japanese businessman, and they met while he was in San Salvador on business, she told me. I stopped drinking my iced tea.

"When I was about to be born, my father flew my mother to Tokyo, and that's where I was born," said Tumiko, cutting potatoes. "My father's wife helped deliver me."

She relayed the story with a cool comportment, as if everyone had parents who were a Central American revolutionary and a Japanese corporate executive married to another woman. After Tumiko's birth, her mother returned to El Salvador, where she was eventually murdered in her San Salvador home, the victim of civil war. But before Tumiko's mother was killed, she and her Japanese businessman produced a second daughter. Tumiko never met her mother and has never met her sister, a woman named Karen Rodriguez.

Tumiko's early years were spent in Japan, where she was raised by her father and her German-born stepmother, and for a time she was shuttled off to her paternal grandparents in Thailand. But when they were killed in an airplane crash, she returned to Tokyo, where she lived until she left for college. Her father sent her to Mexico City, where she began a degree in psychology.

One year, during a summer break, she worked at a bread

stand in an open-air market in Tapachula, in the Mexican state of Chiapas. Across the loaves of bread that summer day in 1987, she spotted her future husband, who was on a Mexican vacation. Paul also noticed Tumiko. The bread stand's owner saw them gazing at each other and, pointing to the two, used the universal language of hand motions to suggest they marry. Tumiko nodded "yes." Paul, a reserved Minnesotan, smiled. They dated for the two weeks Paul remained in Chiapas, and then he returned to his McElmo Canyon home. But a long-distance romance was born.

The two corresponded for three years, after which they decided Tumiko would move to Colorado so they could marry. Then Paul decided to move them to Los Angeles, to make the naturalization process easier for Tumiko and her son, Hoshi, from a failed marriage to a Mexican army officer. Paul found odd jobs and Tumiko worked in restaurants and as a nanny for Mark Hamill, the actor who played Luke Skywalker in the movie *Star Wars*. On some days, Harrison Ford visited his friend and then drove Tumiko down the Malibu canyon where Hamill lived and dropped her off at the bus station. Tumiko enjoyed Los Angeles, but Paul increasingly missed Montezuma County. After a year, the Murphys returned to rural Colorado, where the young family moved into Paul's simple stone home on five acres.

Their canyon home was a respite from traffic-choked Los Angeles, but the couple worked harder in Montezuma County to make ends meet. Paul worked two jobs in stretches, as a detention officer at the Montezuma County Jail and as a self-employed businessman who sold prepaid memberships in a company that provided legal advice. Tumiko worked as a caregiver at a private agency that served developmentally disabled adults. For Tumiko, the effort to stretch a dollar was overshadowed by the dark side of small-town life that Sinclair Lewis had written about nearly a century before. Not much, it seemed, had changed in a small town's psyche.

I thought back twenty years to my first reporting job at the *Brownwood Bulletin* in my native Texas. The town of 22,000 had sizeable African-American and Hispanic populations, but you never knew it by reading the voice of central Texas. White people made all the news. When a black person died, the owner of the funeral home that handled the minority community came by the paper to drop off the death notice. But he didn't use the front door. Instead, he came to the paper's employee entrance at the side of the building. Unsophisticated at twenty-two, I nevertheless found the side door delivery of death notices for African-Americans bizarre.

Two decades later, it seemed, small-town life was only slightly better, and that shouldn't have surprised me given the problems urban areas have with race. But I was nonetheless taken aback.

"Some white people just stare at me," said Tumiko, whose heritage wasn't exactly embraced, or understood, by some Cortezians. Others looked at her, then quickly looked away. Others looked right through her. The friendliest town in the West was amiable only up to a point.

Paul arrived as Tumiko put the last of the vegetables into the bubbling pot of chicken soup, and joined in the conversation. "So many people are moving here, that old-timers just have to deal with it," said Paul, who shared his own stories about life in Cortez. He remembered an African-American friend he had in town whom locals routinely referred to as "the nigger"; the man ultimately returned to California. Over the years, Cortez had been home to a handful of black families, but most of them, like Paul's friend, never stayed very long. They left as quietly as they arrived.

Although some Cortezians had complained mightily about how the movie *Blazing Saddles* portrayed rural Americans, new Montezuma County residents realized Hollywood's portrayal wasn't without merit. Racial slurs rolled off the tongues of some locals with the same ease as the actors in the movie.

There was something else about the unbridled racism that was off-putting. This was the rugged West, where individualism was prized nearly above all else. You could be whatever you wanted to be, live how you wanted to live, and people left you alone. If that was really true, I thought, then Tumiko Murphy and other people of color, the urban people moving to rural America, even the gays and lesbians should have been able to make their way without the stares, the comments, the discomfiting feelings they sometimes encountered. If new residents harbored dreams of an expansive country where they could be free, reality suggested otherwise.

"'Jew you down' is part of the regular vocabulary here," said Mike Fernandez, who moved to a small farm outside Cortez from the Denver area four years earlier. "I was in a store in Dolores, and I heard the clerks say 'nigger this' and 'nigger that' with no shame. That's the way it is here." Other new, mostly urban residents were stunned to hear "Chink" or "Chinaman" to describe the town's small but noticeably growing Asian population, and "spic" and "wetback" used to describe Hispanics.

I didn't have to wait long to experience the town's sensibilities firsthand. While interviewing a community leader about Cortez's economic history, he broke the ice with a joke as I sat down in his office.

"What do you get when you cross a Mexican and a Mormon?" he asked.

"I don't know," I replied.

"A basement full of stolen groceries," he said, chortling at his humor.

He was the only one laughing. He didn't realize that sitting on the other side of his desk was a second generation Mexican-American. I didn't challenge him because, very simply, he had information I needed.

As toxic as I found some of the local attitudes, an especially harsh level of racism was reserved for the Native Americans, who knew which Cortez restaurants and stores welcomed them and which ones did not. They avoided the businesses that did not, in effect practicing an economic boycott of sorts. But Native

Americans couldn't completely avoid Cortez. They did have to shop somewhere, and though many shopped in Durango and Farmington, Cortez was still more convenient, if inhospitable.

White Cortezians, of course, denied they were being hostile or inhospitable, even though they accepted personal checks from white customers while rejecting checks that displayed addresses from Toawoc, the Ute Mountain Ute reservation eleven miles west of Cortez. Some merchants said they were only protecting themselves, that Native Americans more than others had a history of bouncing checks. This helped explain why Native Americans, more than any other local minority group, were required by some businesses to show additional identification before their checks were accepted. But that was only if they were served at all.

One day at lunch, Teresa Blakney and her daughter, Cassie, dined at a truck stop and were stunned at what transpired. A bus of Native American women and a few men disembarked at the restaurant, shopped in its modest gift store, and then waited to be seated. They were turned away by one of the restaurant's employees, saying, "We can't serve you because we're expecting a big lunch crowd." The restaurant, Teresa noticed, was largely empty. The thirty or so Native Americans boarded the bus and left.

"I thought, 'Oh my God, I can't believe they are asking them to leave,'" said Teresa, remembering the incident. "Another woman was sitting at the bar with friends, and she turned to her friends and said, 'Can you believe they're asking them to leave?' I'm sure the Native Americans regret buying anything in the gift shop."

Such slights were so common that Native Americans could count on them like clockwork, but they drew a line with their children. In cooperation with the Montezuma-Cortez School District, the reservation selected three Ute Mountain Ute monitors who had license to wander the schools. Their job was to help white teachers bridge the cultural differences with Native American children.

Donitta Labato, one of the monitors, sometimes lingered outside a classroom's door. What she heard did not please her. On
many occasions, she heard the teacher talk to the Native American children in very stern ways, while addressing the white children more warmly. "When I walked in, there would be this look
on their faces, 'Uh-oh, here she comes,'" she said. "Then their
tone would change immediately. They were nicer to the children.
Their whole demeanor changed. Then I would leave, and the
teacher would start talking mean to them again."

Montezuma County, however, didn't have a lock on narrow
views. In the fall of 1999, several black families from Oakland
moved to a northern California rural community, lured by less
crime, better schools, and affordable housing. Almost immediately, the *Oakland Tribune* reported, one black family woke up to
find a cross chemically burned on its front lawn. Other families
were harassed. Within weeks of arriving, some of the families returned to Oakland.

But attitudes were changing, or were at least being driven un-
derground, in Montezuma County. A large billboard on the road
that led into Cortez advertised the Tomahawk Motel, with its
promise that "Our Prices Won't Scalp You." For several years,
and without success, the Ute Mountain Ute tribe had requested
the motel's owner to remove the offensive sign. The owners finally removed the offending slogan in the spring of 2001, about
six months after the head of the federal Bureau of Indian Affairs
apologized to Native Americans for the agency's "legacy of
racism and inhumanity." The wire story was prominently displayed on the second page of the *Cortez Journal.*

*A*s *Tumiko quietly made her way* through the minefield of attitudes in her new hometown, both she and Paul were glad to have
a school like Battle Rock. When a student one day asked Stephen
for a recommendation on a book to read, Stephen suggested the

biography of Mary McLeod Bethune, the daughter of former slaves who founded the Florida college that bears her name. Tumiko drew solace in the fact that Hoshi, at least, didn't have to deal with the local mindset she encountered. Well, not at school anyway.

That night after dinner, we moved to the front yard, where Paul built a small campfire just off their circular gravel driveway. Hoshi cooked marshmallows as the sweet smoke from the burning cedar floated into an overcast sky, obscuring a full moon. From their front yard, they could see a canyon in the midst of change.

"The traffic has picked up tenfold since I moved here twenty years ago," said Paul, as he gazed down the canyon road illuminated in the headlights or taillights of traffic.

What once was an occasional vehicle through the canyon was now perhaps a dozen cars in an hour, often more, as city dwellers and people from Cortez snapped up the canyon's land. Paul had purchased his property for $1,200 an acre in 1978, a tidy sum back then, and now a single acre in the canyon sold for an average of $20,000, sometimes more.

"I'm glad I bought when I did," Paul said, "because I couldn't afford to today."

The couple's new urban neighbors introduced more than heavier traffic and higher land prices. They brought, more often than not, more-enlightened attitudes about race and ethnicity. "There are still a lot of ignorant people, but they are just having to deal with all the different people moving here," said Paul, adding another chunk of wood to the fire. "Most people are prejudiced in one way or another. It's probably the same here as it is in other places. That's just the way this country is. But it will change."

Nearly a decade after moving to McElmo Canyon, Tumiko still felt the weight of the stares, but she also noticed they were less frequent in the supermarket, at the post office, on Main Street. "Since I've moved here it has gotten better," she said.

She felt that a small community was a better place to raise children, but she still missed urban life. She had told Paul that she wanted to return to a city when their children were grown. She yearned for Los Angeles, where she was just another face in the crowd.

Chapter 10

Getting Along

The fire crackled and hissed as a cold, stiff wind blew through the Sticker Patch on the eve of the school's annual barbecue. Stephen stood at the edge of the playground and nursed the fire blazing six feet below. Earlier in the week, during recesses and after school, he had excavated the pit and then covered the bottom with cottonwood logs heavy with tar that helped feed the fire. Then he added limbs and trunks of peach and apple trees, hardwoods that would burn longer and simmer the meat and vegetables Susan prepared inside the school.

Listening to a Tina Turner CD on a boom box, Susan sliced acorn and butter squash and potatoes and seasoned three slabs of pork, two briskets, and five turkeys. She wrapped everything in foil and waited for Stephen to announce the fire was ready. The meat and vegetables were cooked overnight in the pit.

"This is a lot of work," I volunteered.

"It sure is," said Stephen, as he poked the burning tree trunks and limbs in the pit. Preparing for the barbecue was an all-night affair few others besides the Hansons experienced. Over the years, not many parents had offered to help. As Stephen stoked the fire, he watched the flames; he was lost in thought. Then he cocked his ear, listening to mournful cries over the rushing wind.

"Coyotes," he said, zipping up his jacket. I turned my ear in the same direction and listened as the wind blew from the direction of the Battle Rock Cemetery, its headstones illuminated by a full moon. Either Stephen had very good hearing or I was going deaf. I hadn't heard a thing.

Stephen rarely looked tired, but he did just then in the shiver of the night. His mind was locked on a turn of events that had simmered between Kayla and her two classmates and finally bubbled to the surface earlier that week. This wasn't a problem that a session in the cloakroom could fix.

Kayla had been taunted, then ignored, by the two classmates during the fall, and the girl had finally had enough. Debbie, a tall, solidly built girl, was particularly adept at taunting Kayla at a game called four square, in which players stood in four painted squares and bounced the ball to each other. The ball had to land within the lines of the four large squares, and the school's version of the game was played competitively. Debbie was tall and athletic. She pushed the ball beyond Kayla, who did not possess her classmate's agility.

"Why are you doing this?" Kayla exclaimed one day at recess after Debbie had intentionally pushed the ball into a corner that Kayla couldn't begin to reach. Debbie elevated the competition into meanness when she didn't like someone. Debbie and Connie had then frozen out Kayla for months, sitting together on the bus ride to Farmington and on other field trips. They ignored her at lunch or condemned her to a single turn at four square. When Kayla tried to join their conversations, the girls simply walked away. The rift turned Kayla's last year at Battle Rock into a lonely one; the two classmates were the only other older girls in the school. Kayla ultimately gave up on her classmates, but not before writing a letter to them both. She gave them and Stephen a copy of the letter one morning.

The girls were still reading Kayla's letter when I arrived at school that morning. As I took my place at the third-grade table next to Tim, Kayla quietly came up to me to tell me she had given the girls her note. Kayla's letter, written on stationery with a jelly-bean background, put into words the pain she felt.

> I have been thinking a lot lately about our friendship, how it has been kind of broken apart. Now I'm not trying to be mean. I just want to express how I've felt for the past few weeks.
>
> I have felt left out. Don't get me wrong I am very glad that the two of you are friends. I could think of a lot more things that have hurt me the last few weeks, but seeing it in writing is more than I can deal with. I don't think you guys know that you are emotionally hurting me, but I sometimes cry when I think about it. I think you guys are two of my best friends, but I wish you could feel the same about me. I liked it the way it was before all of this started to happen. Your friend no matter what, Kayla.

The letter ultimately did little to repair the ruptured friendship between the three girls. Such matters were the stuff of growing up, and initially Stephen could only stand on the sidelines as he tried to make sense of the discord. Stephen had little patience for the immaturity of the two girls, who had been left far behind by Kayla in the quality and clarity of her schoolwork and, apparently, her maturity. Stephen felt bad for Kayla, but he had no evidence of the treatment outlined in the one-page letter. The girls were crafty enough to taunt Kayla when the teacher wasn't looking. When he came into the school from watching the fire, he broached the topic with Susan.

"That's terrible," Susan exclaimed after she heard the story.

"It's part of growing up," said Stephen. "And who knows? This experience may be key in making her a great writer. She's well ahead of those girls. It's a school-age issue."

"But you never forget it," Susan responded. "It stays with you all your life. It was brave of her to write that letter."

"More adults ought to do that," Stephen agreed. Susan just shook her head as the two fell silent.

At 4 A.M., the logs in the barbecue pit comfortably red and the darkness crowding us, I helped the Hansons lower three chicken-wire containers holding the meat and vegetables into the fire, stacking them on top of each other. Then Stephen covered the pit with a piece of plywood and began shoveling dirt around the edges and finally on the plywood. They stood nearby to make sure no steam escaped from the now completely covered pit. Then they went back into the school, unrolled their sleeping bags, and went to sleep. I drove back to Cortez, finally getting into bed just past 5 A.M.

At noon the next day, looking surprisingly fresh after staying up most of the night, Stephen and Susan carved the turkeys, beef, and pork and served up the roasted vegetables. They kept the serving line, heaped with steaming well-seasoned food, moving at an efficient clip, even as they both carried on multiple conversations with parents, their friends, and each other.

As a fund-raiser, the barbecue raised more than $1,000 for the school's projects and trips, more of it raised from those who bought tickets without attending than from those who showed up. One student sold $400 worth of tickets in the first week of ticket sales; other buyers, when they read about the Battle Rock barbecue in the local paper, sent in contributions that often exceeded the $10 ticket price.

The barbecue also served as a rare community gathering, one of the few times during the year when everyone, rural and urban, got together in the rapidly changing canyon. The place probably could have used more of these events to bring the community together, but three years after the Botticelli culture war, some residents still viewed each other warily. People could, and did, forgive. But no one ever forgot.

Old wounds—and there were plenty of them in a place like McElmo Canyon—were set aside this day on the Sticker Patch, which held an overflowing crowd under a deep-blue autumn sky. A local performer who looked a lot like Willie Nelson warbled country tunes. He was, in fact, a member of an association of performers who patterned their acts after the country-and-western artist. The tunes floated over the playground.

The performer launched into an enthusiastic rendition of "On the Road Again" as I made my way through the line, greeting Stephen and Susan, who were assisted in the serving, finally, by some parents. I saw a table of urban transplants who now called the canyon home, and I joined them. I immediately knew I had made the wrong decision; though it was a warm day, the reception was icy.

"All I ever hear is country-western music here," complained one urban woman, her plate overflowing with turkey, squash, and a baked potato. She sat across from a couple. At the end of the table sat other canyon residents, none of whom had children in the school but who nonetheless came out to support Stephen Hanson and the one-room school. No one at the table was a native of the canyon. When one woman excused herself to have a cigarette, I joined her.

"Oh, such cliques," she said, as we took drags of our cigarettes, hidden by the trucks and sport utility vehicles in the school parking lot. "That family doesn't get along with that family, and that other family is hateful. They don't like me, but I don't care. I'm not staying long. I just came for Stephen and Susan and the children."

I didn't know the families at all, but I knew enough about the canyon three months into my year to realize that it was a contentious place. I also knew about the histories of the families the woman talked about because other people had already spilled embarrassing details about them. I wasn't sure I wanted to meet them. We finished our cigarettes, and she left.

When I returned to the Sticker Patch, I looked at the table where I had been sitting. Several of the people had canceled interviews with me upon my arrival three months earlier. Even though I had seen them several times since in town, at the grocery store or at the post office, they still barely acknowledged me, if at all. I decided I wasn't interested in dealing with them dealing with me. I moved to another table to sit with a family whose home I had already visited. In that afternoon, I took in my first full measure of the canyon community's personality that Cortezians had warned me about. I decided again that Stephen deserved every penny he earned.

The barbecue was a study in canyon politics and the divisions. As with most interactions that involve people, a very small group left messes everyone else had to deal with. Like the Kayla situation. The discord between the three girls had reached John and Brenda Burns, Kayla's parents, of course. John wanted to pull his daughter out of the school immediately. But Brenda was more inclined, like Kayla, to stick it out.

"Give it three weeks," Stephen told the Burnses.

John and Brenda looked more hurt than Kayla, who looked plenty bruised walking by herself on the Sticker Patch. Debbie's and Connie's parents were there, too, and all the parents successfully avoided one another—no small feat in a small community where folks routinely bumped into each other on Main Street whether they wanted to or not.

That night, Susan and Stephen talked more about Kayla. Susan was regularly an attentive sounding board for her husband, and she was, more often than not, proactive in her recommendations.

"You have to talk to those girls and their parents, Stephen," Susan said, as she opened a can of cranberry sauce. In the crush of the day, they hadn't eaten, and they sat down to leftovers of turkey, squash, homemade rolls, and martinis, which Susan euphemistically called Stephen's "olive salad."

"I will talk to them," said Stephen, who methodically studied situations before making decisions.

"That poor child," Susan said.

The Hansons settled in their comfortably furnished home warmed by the wood-burning stove and watched the first game of the 1999 World Series, between the New York Yankees and the Atlanta Braves. By midnight, following the Yankees' come-from-behind win, Stephen and Susan trudged upstairs to their bedroom. The Kayla situation, Stephen decided, would have to play itself out.

Months later, I encountered John Burns after Sunday morning services at the First Assembly of God. "We hear all sorts of things going on at the school," he told me. "How do you think it's going?"

I sighed. There was no escaping John's question.

Stephen ran a tight school, I told John, and the teacher was forced to discipline students several times a day. "He can't be everywhere," I told John.

John seemed to agree.

The conversation underscored one thing: as hard as I tried to mind my own affairs, to remain independent as a newcomer, the politics of a small community didn't allow it. Parents interrogated me about school topics large and small, including the behavior of their children. I had, in a handful of months, come to know several families well enough that they felt comfortable asking me sensitive and pointed questions. Their queries made me uneasy.

Kayla's situation wasn't the only instance in which I was interrogated. As the behind-the-scenes battle over the quality of the school's academics heated up between Stephen and Kim Lindgren, several parents asked me what was going on at the school. I told them I didn't have a clue; that was the truth, at least early on. But people didn't believe me, because they knew I had been a guest in the Lindgren home many times and they knew I dined often with the Hansons.

   As I drove home that night after the school barbecue and after dining with Stephen and Susan, I discarded another small-town myth. For such a small community, there was more discord than I could have imagined, and it ran deep.

Chapter 11

A Battle Rock
Christmas

There was never a moment's peace now for Stephen as he rushed to give the children their exams, grade essays, and file end-of-semester reports to the local school district. But in the weeks before Thanksgiving, when the weather turned bitterly cold and the summit of the Sleeping Ute Mountain was shrouded by heavy gray clouds, Stephen turned his attention to the most important detail on his calendar: Battle Rock's annual Christmas pageant.

"We're going to do the *Nutcracker Suite,* but there won't be any speaking parts," Stephen told his students one morning as he began putting together the rough beginnings of the Christmas program. "Does everyone know what mime means?"

"What's that?" asked Staton.

"It means no talking. We're going to act it out."

Kayla was assigned the task of reading the script, her steady and clear voice a natural for the job, the teacher decided. Under Stephen's direction, the children took their positions. Tim was assigned the role of a toy soldier, Staton and the younger boys were assigned the role of rats, and Hoshi and Harold were cast in supporting roles. Stephen pulled the children here and there, arranging their bodies to size up the scale of the stage that would be built in the coming week. As Stephen continued assigning the children parts in the play, the giggling and laughter grew louder and louder.

"Quiet! Please!" bellowed Stephen in his teacher's voice. He turned around from the makeshift stage, where he had been arranging some of the children, and looked at the guilty children. The room was silent for only a few minutes before the talking, giggles, and then laughter erupted once more.

"Please. Quiet," he said, more earnestly.

The teacher always felt pressure when assembling the school's traditional and much anticipated Christmas program. "Parents expect perfection, and children still believe in magic," he said at the end of a long day. In time, the rehearsals became more polished as the children became familiar with their roles and cues.

Stephen had his hands full, but so did Wendy Watkins. The school's part-time music teacher had started the older students on recorders earlier in the fall, and the rudimentary scales gradually evolved into full tunes. Slowly, the jagged versions of "Jingle Bells" gave way to slightly smoother renditions of the song as Wendy cajoled her young musicians to fifth- and sixth-grade perfection. I noticed the students improving, but their progress wasn't nearly fast enough for a music teacher with exacting standards—not when the Christmas pageant was less than a month away.

"No, that's a rest!" she said one day, raising her voice at Harold in exasperation when the students went through a practice run of "Jingle Bells."

"Have you been practicing?" she asked the boy.

Harold obviously had not. Some of the other children were clearly not up to speed either, but none of them equaled Harold in blowing notes in places where notes weren't supposed to be heard. Wendy surveyed the class.

"I don't know what I'm going to do with you guys," she said with more than a hint of frustration in her voice.

Tears gathered in Harold's eyes. He took off his glasses and then pulled his black *Star Wars* T-shirt up over his face until only the top of his curly blond hair was visible. He then returned his glasses to his nose protruding through the T-shirt and put his hands over his glasses. His face disappeared so quickly that within seconds the entire class sat staring at Harold's head wrapped up in his T-shirt. Wendy was at her wit's end. For one of the few occasions all fall, she was rendered speechless. The silence was deafening.

"Poor guy," Kayla mouthed quietly.

The other children looked away, at the ceiling, at the floor, everywhere but at Harold, who sat quietly in the middle of the room.

"That's okay," Wendy finally said. "We'll work something out."

After she dismissed the class, she wondered aloud about Harold, so quickly moved to tears about anything and everything, it seemed. When the children had left the teacherage and were safely out of earshot, she turned to me.

"Am I being horrible?" she asked.

"No," I said. "Standards are standards at any age."

This was more than a teacher upset over a student's lack of preparedness. The moment spoke volumes about schools holding students to a measure of competency. The 1983 report *A Nation at Risk,* which decried American schools slipping into mediocrity, sounded the alarm first, and subsequent white papers bemoaned students graduating from every level of school without mastering the basics. Whether it was math, science, literature, or a host of other topics, students just weren't being pressed, weren't achieving, weren't prepared. Some of the reasons were, by now, widely known: disintegration of families, poverty and hunger, the advent of social promotion. But in a country school, in five minutes of awkwardness between teacher and student, standards and mediocrity, Wendy Watkins had drawn a line in the sand. The reasons why Harold wasn't prepared almost didn't matter; she knew, as everyone else in the community did, that a single father was raising Harold and that the boy sometimes went to an empty home.

Wendy was a compassionate teacher, and she empathized with her students. But once the door to the teacherage was closed and music class began, she held all her students to the same standard, no matter their circumstances. She felt she owed her students that much. Other Battle Rock teachers pushed their students, but no one tested the mettle of her pupils more than Wendy. When they left her classes, they knew the difference between a whole note and a half note, the values given each rest, and they knew about the lives of composers she introduced them to, from Beethoven to Tchaikovsky.

Before she left Battle Rock that day, Wendy decided that she wasn't being unreasonable. But something had to be done about the boy, because she wasn't about to put her good name and reputation as one of the best music teachers in the Four Corners region behind a poor performance. Dispositions were stretched thin in the closing weeks of the fall semester, which is why Stephen, Wendy, and even the students breathed collective sighs of relief when the calendar approached and then settled on Thanksgiving.

*T*he bullet grazed the turkey's head.

"Oh, man, you missed!" Hoshi yelled to his father, Paul, as both of them peered through the brown slats of the coop holding the hefty turkey, which tottered from the near miss.

I stood a few feet behind Paul and closed my eyes when he pulled the trigger. Shivering on the cold and blustery day, I wondered why the Murphys didn't go to the grocery store for a turkey like the majority of good Americans. Paul steadied his rifle between the slats of the small pen and took aim. I looked away and this time felt myself grimacing as Paul shot a second, then a third time. I turned and looked into the pen. The turkey was still standing, its will immense. But in about two or three minutes, it staggered, then dropped to the ground in a heap of feathers and a small cloud of dust. Hoshi and I peered through the slats of the pen and watched the turkey's body convulse until it was still.

Hoshi retrieved the turkey, then Tumiko, Paul's wife, took over. In a wind so strong it bent the nearby trees, she hung the bird from her clothesline by its feet, slit its throat, and then watched the blood drain from the twenty-pound bird she had raised from a chick six months before.

Hoshi, a curious sixth-grade boy, poked at the turkey.

"Hoshi, get away," she said, shooing her son away from the turkey, which was, at this point, quite dead. "It has suffered enough."

Harvesting a turkey was nothing new for the Murphys. For several years, the family had ordered at least four turkey chicks from a local supplier, and despite a high mortality rate due to illness and hungry dogs, Paul and Tumiko managed to coax at least one of them to adulthood and ultimately onto their Thanksgiving table. Both of them disdained the commercial farm-raised turkeys because of chemicals pumped into the birds to spur growth and weight. The Murphys had fed natural grains to their turkeys.

"It tastes much better," Paul told me, as he dragged the bird into the kitchen a half hour after it was killed. "Wait and see."

Paul put the turkey in the sink. Tumiko put her shoulder-length dark brown hair in a turban, rolled up her sleeves, and got down to business. Getting to this point—a dead twenty-pound turkey in a kitchen sink—required a strong constitution in more ways than one.

People became attached to turkey chicks, and there were plenty of stories about how chicks ultimately became pets. This happened one year to Wendy the music teacher. She bought and raised two turkey chicks, naming them Thanksgiving and Christmas to remind her family why they were part of the Watkins household. When Wendy finally read a book for instructions on how to butcher and clean a turkey, the holidays came and went, and Thanksgiving and Christmas still puttered around Wendy's yard. The Murphys avoided that danger. When I asked if the bloodied turkey in the sink had a name, Tumiko shook her head "no." "We didn't want to get attached to it," she told me.

If the prospect of butchering didn't send someone scurrying to a supermarket for a frozen turkey, then that of cleaning certainly would have. Tumiko took the handles of a large pot of boiling water and dumped it on the bird to scald it. I helped her pluck off the feathers, which came off easily enough, but a short lifetime of scratching the ground and rolling around in the dirt did not make for an inviting aroma. The kitchen smelled something awful. Disemboweling the turkey required a strong stomach, and Tumiko's slight head cold was a blessing. I was not so fortunate, so I breathed through my mouth.

"This is not my favorite part," she said with her characteristic calm voice. She took a large knife and sliced through the turkey's breastbone, then emptied the turkey's body organ by organ. She put the giblets, destined for dressing, in a pot of boiling water. The neck and other turkey parts she set aside for use in other meals. The Murphys didn't waste an ounce of food.

The wind outdoors whistled as Paul came in from scouring the landscape for an herb to make his wife some tea. The brew, called Mormon tea, had medicinal qualities, but Tumiko liked the way it tasted. As we sat down to take in the tea's restorative qualities, I looked past Tumiko. The turkey's long legs stuck out of the sink.

On a cloudy Thanksgiving Day, with a strong wind rushing through the canyon's corridor, the smell of roasting turkey drifted through the Murphy home. Paul made good on his promise. The turkey minus all the chemicals was indeed better eating than a commercially raised turkey. There were potatoes, dressing, salad, and pumpkin and key lime pie with cream. The family's guests appeared with more food, another salad, and a hot chili dip. I looked out over the spread assembled on Paul and Tumiko's table and realized that virtually everything that simmered in pots and serving dishes had been grown either by them or their guests. The prayer offered by Paul, who thanked God for blessing the family with fruits of the land, took on special meaning that day.

*T*eresa Blakney *approached Stephen* about entering a school float in the Cortez Christmas parade.

"Enter the parade," he replied. "But I want nothing to do with it." The teacher knew from experience that the project was time-consuming and that the work ultimately fell on a small number of people, namely him.

Teresa thought for a moment and then decided the school had a reputation to uphold. Battle Rock had won first place the previous year, and a few weeks before the mid-December parade, she began preparations to defend the school's honor. With her husband, Bill, playing her lieutenant, the two built a wood frame that resembled a sleigh with its characteristic curves. They wrapped the frame, which sat on a long trailer, in chicken wire and then began the tedious task of stuffing white tissue in the wire-wrapped skeleton. On the back of the sleigh, they used bright-red tissue paper to spell out *Battle Rock,* the letters leaning and wobbling a bit.

On most afternoons and mornings when Teresa wasn't at Battle Rock or working behind the counter at the liquor store, she was laboring over the float, parked on the street next to her mother's home. In wind and frigid temperatures, even in a light snowfall, she pushed tissue paper through the wire. Sometimes Bill helped, sometimes her mother. On rare occasions, other parents showed up. As she pressed the tissue paper into the chicken wire, Teresa figured the float had a good chance to win an award from the local realtor group that sponsored the Cortez Festival of Lights Christmas Parade.

On parade night, the temperature plunging to twenty-two degrees, the Blakneys and Hansons taped twinkling white lights to the float. As the children arrived to take their places on the float, I watched the couples frantically making last-minute adjustments to the giant sleigh. A truck disguised as a reindeer pulled the float. Huge antlers crowned the truck's cab, which was also topped by a red swirling light. Some of the children dressed like traditional toys and storybook characters; others donned more contemporary costumes. One child dressed like a computer, a medium-sized box hanging around his midsection with knobs and aluminum foil masquerading as a screen; another dressed like the Tin Man in *The Wizard of Oz*. The children took their places, as the last-minute arrivals scurried to get on the top of the float.

The driver started the engine and then lurched across the intersection, the back of the trailer groaning and scraping the dips in the road. The children bounced backward, then forward, and then they were off to take their place in the parade line. Stephen, Susan, and I walked two blocks to find a place on Main Street, already three to five people deep. Small towns always turn out for a celebration, and Cortez was no exception.

The forty-five-minute parade displayed Montezuma County at its rural holiday best. Illuminated plastic figures of Joseph, Mary, and Baby Jesus sat in a front-end loader. People applauded. Several dogs, wearing make-believe antlers, their bodies draped in garland and lights, drew hearty applause. Goats in tinsel bleated down Main Street. Eighteen-wheel rigs representing local businesses and decorated in lights rumbled down Main Street, blowing their loud horns. Horses in holiday garland clip-clopped before the throng, leaving the requisite souvenirs on the street that the two marching bands deftly avoided.

Midway through the parade, Battle Rock's float glided down Main Street. Kayla, sporting earmuffs, and two of her classmates marched in front of the float, carrying a colorful school banner:

BATTLE ROCK, 85 Years of Christmas, 1915–2000

Despite Stephen's reluctance to work on the school's Christmas float, he made the banner one day at lunch by carefully drawing the letters with a black marker on a roll of white cloth. The children filled in the letters with colored markers, creating the banner's kaleidoscope effect.

"Ooooh, honey, it looks wonderful," exclaimed Susan, nursing a cup of hot chocolate. Stephen, a video camera to his face, managed to free one hand to wave to the children.

"Hello, Mr. Hanson!" several of them hollered, as the float passed by us. Battle Rock's entry, judging from the applause, was as popular as the "reindeer" and goats. Later that night, as the Hansons warmed themselves by the fire in their home, the phone rang. The caller was an ebullient Teresa. Stephen complimented her.

"She nailed it," Stephen later told Susan, as he sipped on a martini.

The float didn't win a prize, but Teresa had done her part. Now it was the teacher's turn to produce the school's annual holiday play, the mimed version of the *Nutcracker.*

The day before the performance, Stephen scheduled a dress rehearsal at Madison House, a Cortez nursing home nestled on a tree-lined street. I came to watch the performance and selected a seat in the midst of the home's residents. The room was packed for the play, during which I noticed several residents napping. But when the children sang "Bicycle Built for Two," the "Sidewalks of New York," and other songs that were popular tunes for many of the oldest residents in their youth, the residents awakened. One woman tapped on her oxygen tank as the rousing tunes warmed the room. After the program, residents walked back slowly to their rooms, some of them silently mouthing "Thank you" to Stephen, who also bumped into Mary Taylor. At 104, she was one of the older residents at the nursing home and a former teacher at Battle Rock in the 1920s. She thanked Stephen, and the two teachers chatted amicably for a few minutes before she returned to her room. Stephen was relieved the conversation was a short one.

"She probably would have told me to cut my hair if we had talked much longer," he told Teresa, smiling.

The following night, nearly a hundred people—parents, grand-parents, aunts, uncles, siblings, and friends—squeezed into the one-room school and witnessed the fruits of rehearsal and end-less weeks of anxiety for Stephen and Wendy. I sat next to Chris and Andrea Jeter and near John and Brenda Burns. The parents beamed at the flawless performances that night, utterly oblivious to the stress and strain of producing a school play and concert. Wendy, the ever resourceful music teacher, even found a solution for Harold, whose efficiency on the recorder had not improved in the days leading up to the concert. The boy beamed on the stage with the rest of his classmates as he tapped on a tambourine.

At the end of the program, the children exchanged presents, and the schoolroom became a colorful commotion of wrapping paper and exclamations of surprise. Stephen received several gifts, including an attractive brown briefcase purchased with contributions from all the children. One of the other presents came from Harold.

The wrapping paper held an oversized mug for soup or coffee, and Harold had finished it off himself at a crafts store with a per-sonal message. "You're the best teacher I ever had," Harold wrote in his uneven penmanship. Stephen was touched until he thought about it. "I'm the *only* teacher he's ever had," he told Su-san, as we drove the dark canyon road toward Cortez. They laughed as the lights of the town appeared on the horizon.

Part II

Chapter 12

A Canyon Winter

*D*ays into the spring term, Stephen was inundated with work. His teacher's table had limited space, and the new semester had already generated so much paperwork that it buried the books on his desk. He looked above for help. A clothesline ran nearly the length of the one-room school and was tied to another line at the far end of the room. The thin cords, used in past years to hang curtains for school plays or to create smaller classrooms, produced an off-centered T, as well as an airborne filing system. The teacher used clothespins to hang important or urgent paperwork.

By the end of the second week, the clothesline held as many sheets of paper as it had at the end of the fall term. As Stephen launched the final months of school, he sometimes felt as if he had had no break at all, no Christmas trip to sunny Los Angeles with Susan to visit her parents. Stephen looked only nominally rested.

"It's never ending," he told me on the Sticker Patch one day. As he drank soup from a mug, we watched the children play on a cold day when the naked cottonwoods near the school rattled in the occasional bursts of wind.

Whenever the part-time teachers took over the classes, Stephen pressed to finish the paperwork, much of it related to Battle Rock's charter school status. Charter school legislation gave communities more freedom to fashion schools that mirrored their sensibilities. But without a central administration office to manage even a small school like Battle Rock, Stephen and his aide, Teresa, were forced to process requests of every kind from the Montezuma–Cortez School District. They also paid the school's bills, ordered their own office equipment, made their own reservations and travel plans for the school's trips. There was a price for Battle Rock's independence, and it hung, literally, over Stephen's head.

Between the administrative details, Stephen dispatched emails to other rural teachers, or "lifelines," as he called them. In late January he began making preparations to meet his email colleagues at a three-day meeting of the Colorado Rural Charter School Network, which Stephen had helped create. The meeting of six rural schools scheduled for February brought together kindred souls, other teachers like Stephen who taught in one-room and two-room schools in Colorado's rugged outback.

"No way would I be teaching in a one-room school without this network of teachers," he said at the end of that day. "It is too difficult to do it alone. The network makes difficult work somewhat easier because we can support each other." As Stephen drove home that gray afternoon, he was unaware that he would need the support of his cyberspace colleagues in a matter of months.

On a cold day when Stephen tackled the papers hanging from his clothesline and the sun lost its battle with a thick bank of clouds, students began a science project designed for the weather. Anne Wright, the school's part-time science and math teacher, launched the students on a lesson that combined science with the environment and then blended the two with a cooking lesson. The canyon's birds were the ultimate beneficiaries.

Grouping older children with younger ones, Anne assembled them in the old teacherage and then divided the students into several groups, giving each one generous portions of lard, corn, and flour. Kayla, the sixth grader with the soft brown hair, guided three younger classmates through the intricacies of measuring lard, flour, and the other ingredients for the birds' winter feast.

Kayla scooped lard into a small saucepan that sat atop a single burner in a corner of the room, and then melted the lard. She turned up her nose as the melting animal fat released an unpleasant odor.

"We can add snake eyes and snake brains," said Skylar, an affable third grader with a toothy smile.

"I'll be the food critic," Kayla added.

Troy and Maya, both first graders, studied the lard as it began to bubble. Skylar scooped up some of the melting lard with a finger and put it in his mouth.

"You're sick!" shrieked Kayla.

"She's going to hurl!" said Skylar, smiling and waiting for Kayla to lose her lunch.

"Gross!" Kayla said, raising her voice. She didn't get sick, but she moved away from the burner as the lard continued its pungent melt.

After Skylar had sampled the goo, Maya and Troy added two cups of corn to the pot and stirred. Much of the corn landed on the floor. Kayla added a cup of whole wheat flour. She then stirred the thickening concoction.

"This looks like poop," said Skylar.

"You are sick!" said Kayla.

"I wish I was a bird," said Maya in a tiny voice.

"It looks like poop!" Troy echoed.

With the mix now cooling, the children took small plastic molds and scooped the melted lard, corn, and flour into the molds and then patted it down. The table and the floor were a mess.

"It looks like snot stew," said Skylar, as he scooped another spoonful of the mix and put it in his mouth. He swallowed the hard corn kernels whole.

Kayla rolled her eyes, Maya made a sour face, and Troy burst into laughter.

The exercise was over in an hour. The cakes, set aside to harden, were later hung from trees and fence posts for the rich variety of birds that called McElmo Canyon home.

Anne had created five groups of students late in the fall, assigning each group the task of studying issues surrounding Montezuma County's wildlife, environment, archeology, water, and economy. Anne and the children braved the blur of winter weather; it snowed, then cleared, then warmed; then the cycle repeated itself. The students' energy levels and attention spans mirrored the winter, ebbing and flowing almost in rhythm with the storms that blew into the canyon.

As inventive as she was with her lessons, Anne conceded that traditional approaches were sometimes best. After several weeks of exploring the county with her students, Anne assembled the fifth and sixth graders for math lessons that had been started during the fall. As the students entered the teacherage one afternoon, Anne wrote several equations on the board and then was forced to dig deep into her reservoir of teaching tricks to complete the lesson.

"We're going to work on fractions, percentages, and decimal points," she announced as they settled into their chairs. They groaned collectively. Debbie, one of the older girls, noticed Kayla wasn't in the math class.

"How come Kayla isn't in the room?" she asked.

Anne sighed.

"Because she is doing algebra," Anne said. "She already knows what we're doing. She has to finish the math book we're on, and she will. She's going to home school next year because that's what she wants to do, and while I'm here, I'm teaching her algebra."

Anne didn't owe Debbie an explanation, but she discovered that full explanations were sometimes necessary on topics that were none of the girl's business. Anne offered the explanations to maintain peace in the class.

But the fifth and sixth graders weren't of a collective mind to embrace fractions, decimals, and percentages on this gray wintry day.

"Do you have any snot rags?" Hoshi asked.

"Here is a *tissue,*" Anne said, passing a box of Kleenex.

Then Debbie interrupted the class again. She wondered aloud why a classmate got a fine-point pen and why she got a marker with a blunt point to use on the plastic-covered work sheets Anne had provided. Sometimes even Debbie's classmates tired of her; they shot her annoyed looks.

"No wonder we don't know fractions, decimals, and percentages!" Anne exclaimed.

To calm them, Anne made them play money bingo. Slowly and skillfully she squeezed out every bit of excess energy that stood in the way of teaching. The students played several rounds of the game until they were quiet. Anne then hit them with percentages, decimals, and fractions.

"What is 24.08 in a fraction?" she asked, looking at Connie.

"Yes, yes, what? What?" the girl answered.

Connie, perhaps, had more difficulty with math than any of her classmates. When the girl supplied an incorrect answer, Anne pulled out bright blue manipulatives in different shapes. She began pulling them apart with the efficiency and skill of a math teacher who had been down this road before.

"Ugh," Debbie moaned.

Anne ignored the girl's comment. She continued working with Connie until she was closer to understanding the concept of converting decimals to fractions.

"Now we'll do some problems," Anne said. "Well, you all have problems. I'm going to give you more."

The children laughed. Even Anne, nursing a cold, managed a smile. She gave the class three subtraction problems involving fractions. Most of the students produced the correct answers, but Connie stumbled on them all.

"A lot of you are still having trouble with fractions," said Anne, looking over the mixed results. Only one student received a perfect score. Battle Rock's small classes allowed Anne to work with students one-on-one, a luxury in large, urban schools. But the personalized in-class tutoring took place only after Anne broke through antimath attitudes. In Connie's case, the teacher faced an uphill battle.

"I hate fractions!" Connie exclaimed as the class ended. "They are evil."

Stephen put the early weeks of the term behind him as he and Susan began packing for a trip to the small Colorado town of Crestone. Serious business was scheduled at the annual meeting of the Colorado Rural Charter School Network, but there was a restorative quality about the meetings. They allowed the rural teachers to lean on each other and gather momentum for the balance of the school year, which, by May, had extracted a pound, or two, of flesh.

Stephen had invited me to join him and Susan on the trip, and I looked forward to a change of scenery from my Sunday drives through Utah. Under February skies that threatened a storm, the Hansons packed warm clothes, extra blankets, and pillows for the four-hour drive to Crestone, a small village built in the shadow of the Sangre de Cristo Mountains.

Leaving Cortez, we traveled on Highway 160 through the San Juan National Forest. As we approached Wolf Creek Pass, the forbidding clouds unleashed a blizzard. Conveniently following a snowplow clearing the road, Stephen steered his Explorer through near whiteout conditions that shrouded the 10,850-foot mountain pass. The pass was arduous driving in any weather, but especially so in a winter storm. I looked out the window at the evergreens, faint profiles in the thick swirl of snow. A snow bank nearly as tall as Stephen's Explorer was the only guard between the road and a drop-off of several hundred feet. Mountain driving, in winter or any other season for that matter, was no easy assignment. On more than one occasion, I read stories in the Denver newspapers about people accidentally driving off or backing off mountain roads. When I read further into the story, the driver was usually from a flat state. And then there were the stories of people who intentionally drove off mountainsides, suicides evidently. There were other dangers, like boulders careening down mountainsides onto motorists. I had read plenty of those stories too.

Remembering those incidents made me uneasy, but there wasn't much to do except enjoy the ride, and I drew some comfort from the fact that Stephen was familiar with Highway 160. He had driven it often during his courtship with his then girlfriend Susan, who lived on the other side of the mountain pass during the year they dated. But even an experienced driver like Stephen had his own stories to tell about mountain driving.

On one trip across Wolf Creek, he helped a friend deliver equipment for an Environmental Protection Agency Superfund cleanup of an abandoned copper mine located in the folds of the San Juan Mountains. The trailer jackknifed, sending the pickup truck careening across the snow-covered road and into a sturdy snow bank. The wall of snow kept the two men from plummeting 1,000 feet to their presumed deaths or at least serious injury. Susan listened quietly, as I stole another look out the window.

"By the grace of God," said Susan, a good Catholic.

"Yes," said Stephen, who also offered that both he and his friend had consumed six cans of beer while making the trip.

"That was smart," said Susan, who didn't typically render

opinions about her husband's pre-Susan life but couldn't pass up the opportunity on this occasion.

The marriage was a second one for both. On a trip to Lake George, Colorado, to visit the rural community's school, Stephen laid eyes on Susan, who ran the tiny school's computer lab. In the next year, they dated, with the teacher making several treks to the mountain community northeast of Colorado Springs. Stephen finally proposed on an outing to Denver. They were married in June 1999 at a friend's McElmo Canyon home, and Susan moved to Cortez. They integrated their families—Stephen's two sons and Susan's son—and added onto the bungalow that Stephen had purchased with extra money he earned working summers as a surveyor with a construction company. In Susan, Stephen had found a partner who was "my life." She supported him in his work at Battle Rock, attending the school's board meetings and field trips, helping with the school barbecue, and accompanying him on business trips to Denver, Colorado Springs, and now, Crestone.

As Stephen guided his Explorer down the other side of the pass, the snow fell more lightly and then disappeared altogether. Four hours after leaving Cortez, a trek that took us through the picturesque towns of Durango and Pagosa Springs and through several tiny settlements that didn't even have traffic signals, we arrived in the San Luis Valley as the sun began to set.

The sprawling valley, framed by the towering Sangre de Cristo Mountains, was a fertile place, made so by an aquifer located so close to the earth's surface that water sometimes collected in pools on the ground. When we finally passed the highway sign for Crestone, Stephen announced our imminent arrival.

"Eeeee-ooooo-eeeee, we're in Crestone," he joked, his voice climbing and descending the scale in an eerie *Twilight Zone* tone, a reference to what many Coloradoans thought of this town of New Age and Eastern-religion devotees.

Multicolored Tibetan prayer flags fluttered from the porches of some homes, while others displayed statues of Buddha in their front yards. The town promised a unique experience, and it didn't disappoint. A flyer on the bulletin board in the Crestone Property Owners Association building, a boxy, tan structure, advertised an early March meeting of "courageous residents who would tell their stories about encounters with UFOs and Extra-Terrestrials." Somehow, the Southern Baptists found themselves here, too, one of the few Western congregations in town. The place could have been Berkeley, California's sister city in the Rocky Mountains for all the eclecticism that alternately made the town a haven for those drawn to its purported spiritual power and a butt of jokes among those who considered themselves more grounded.

The town was no more than a smattering of houses, a combination liquor-restaurant-convenience store and a bed-and-breakfast with a Laundromat. The homes were originally built for high-ranking retired military personnel, and developers intentionally made getting in and out of Crestone more difficult by leaving the roads unpaved.

These days, most of the roads were paved, and few, if any, high-powered military people were residents. It was in Crestone, amid the small plastic statues of E.T. and other alien knick-knacks sold at the town's modest flea market, that rural teachers gathered to discuss the difficulties of keeping a network of country schools open while offering quality education. The organization of six schools enjoyed support from the $300,000 grant it received from the Annenberg Rural Challenge. The schools also received their allotment of state aid, and the combination of both funding sources gave the teachers financial support for ambitious school programs unmatched in most other rural schools and especially fiscally strapped urban systems. Some of the network's schools published their community's only newspaper, while others offered literacy classes and other adult programs. And so when the teachers gathered in Crestone, the meeting was as much a celebration of their work as it was a business gathering.

The meetings began warmly in the Desert Sage Conference Center, but the room became eerily still as one horror story unfolded from ground zero of rural America's makeover. Calamity had befallen Paradox Valley Charter School, school director Renee Owens recounted, illustrating the difficulty of managing a rural school. Renee, thirty-two, began crying as she told how one parent, facing a long jail sentence for several different skirmishes with the law, "threatened to take everyone out," Renee said. "I'm scared!"

Renee wiped tears from her eyes, and when she had composed herself, she told the group her school faced another issue. Because of a bureaucratic snafu, the school hadn't received $25,000 of its budget. Someone hadn't filed the correct papers on time with the local school district, and though the problem was corrected months later, Renee still faced the immediate matter of meeting payroll.

"I don't know how I'm going to pay the staff," she said, bouncing her blond-haired, blue-eyed son, Geronimo, on her knees.

Here, in the supportive confines of the lodge, teachers bared their souls as they talked about their jobs, which took in far more than teaching. Steven Finn, who taught at the Marble Charter School in Marble, Colorado, told his colleagues he had built the ice-skating rink for town residents because no one else could or would. Marble was, perhaps,the most exotic of the tiny communities represented at the meeting. The town earned its name because of a quarry that produced white marble of such quality that it was used in monuments and buildings across the country, including the Lincoln Memorial and the Tomb of the Unknown Soldier in Washington, D.C.

"Sometimes it's very tiring," said Steven, whose Marble school took in kindergarten through third grade.

The other teachers nodded in agreement, as they shared the triumphs and the setbacks that made teaching in a one- or two-room rural school a singular experience. Maybe Crestone's spiritual energy, one teacher volunteered, would help the rural network's schools. Lord knew—or Buddha (this was Crestone, after all)—that some of the schools needed help, she said with a smile. The teachers knew each other so well that they felt comfortable injecting levity, even in the midst of worrisome reports.

The night wasn't all grim. The group learned that Oxford University had accepted Stephen as part of Middlebury College's master's program for rural teachers. Other teachers from the rural charter school network participated in the Middlebury program, but no one from the Colorado group had ever been accepted by Oxford. When the meeting concluded, Stephen's colleagues surrounded him to offer their congratulations.

The Crestone gathering underscored how far some rural schools and their communities had traveled. None of this makeover, however, would have been possible without veteran rural teachers who successfully fought efforts to close their country schools. These teachers didn't benefit from generous grants from deep-pocketed foundations. They didn't have access to graduate degree programs housed at prestigious colleges and universities. Battle Rock's doors were kept open because of the tenacity of a Mormon schoolteacher named Audrey Allmon. She dipped into her own pocket to buy supplies for the school, helped clothe and feed some of the school's poorest children, and in short, devoted the best years of her life to Battle Rock. In her day, she was as closely identified with the one-room school as Stephen Hanson was in the 1990s.

Chapter 13

Audrey

*F*ew people go through life so widely known that they are easily identified by only their first names. Even in Cortez, people usually needed both names to get by. Given these time-honored rules about people and places, I was surprised when I sat down one afternoon with the *Cortez Journal* and noticed a small item buried in the paper. The article announced an upcoming meeting of the Battle Rock 4-H Club and gave the date, time, and address. After the address, set off by parentheses, were two words: *Audrey's house*. Despite all the new faces and names on Main Street, life was that simple if you were Audrey Allmon.

She lived at the head of McElmo Canyon in a two-level manufactured house that, from a distance, looked as if it was constructed of logs. Her home sat at the end of a gravel lane that snaked its way from the canyon road. Next to the house, snuggled against the canyon wall, were several structures, including a garage, a horse stable, and a simple one-room building that served as a community center for the canyon.

At seventy-three she was in amazingly fine shape. She still shoed her own horse, Skipper, and split the large logs for the wood-burning stove that sat in a corner of her living room. The energy she possessed was legendary, and sometimes her drive got the better of her. When she stretched herself too thin, she sometimes suffered from migraine headaches. When she felt one coming on, she turned off the overhead lights in her home and relaxed by the softer glow of a kerosene lamp. The rigorous and no-frills lifestyle kept many longtime canyon residents so fit in their youth that in their advancing years they looked like Audrey Allmon, who, migraines aside, was healthy and lean. "Clean living," Audrey called it.

If Stephen Hanson was Battle Rock's present, Audrey was its past. In her thirty-six years at Battle Rock, a stretch that encompassed a dizzying array of educational theories and reforms, she had educated hundreds of Montezuma County residents and won a string of prizes. A wall in her living room displayed twenty-two awards and citations from every educational and local organization imaginable, including a letter from President Richard M. Nixon congratulating Audrey for her 1973 Colorado Teacher of the Year award. Hanging amid the awards was a subtle watercolor of Battle Rock school, the noble cottonwoods in full, leafy bloom.

She had always known she wanted to teach, she told me when I came to her home the first time. When I arrived, she opened the door and welcomed me as though I was a long-lost friend. The first thing that greeted visitors was a portrait of Jesus, and in her kitchen, a reminder to "Be Humble." She apologized for her home's clutter and for the papers that lay strewn on her kitchen table, where we ate. As someone who had courted clutter all his life, I felt quite at home. We pushed the papers to a corner of the table and dined. She had prepared steak, mashed potatoes, green beans, and salad. The beef, she told me, was from a Battle Rock 4-H cow.

When we finished dinner, we adjourned to her comfortably

furnished living room, warmed by the wood-burning stove. When she began recounting her years as a teacher, I quickly realized that I was listening to a rich oral history of decades gone by, of a school that no longer existed even in the remotest stretches of America.

Launching her career in 1945, following high school graduation, Audrey joined hundreds of other mostly young women taking their places in classrooms vacated by seasoned teachers drafted during World War II or dispatched to wartime assembly lines. They were called sixty-day wonders, their training compressed into a handful of weeks. The new recruits were then sent to the nation's schools with emergency teaching certificates. These quickly minted teachers were young. Audrey was only sixteen when she accepted her first teaching assignment for $1,100 a year in a one-room school in Montezuma County. But she and others like her also entered a profession that still had respect and relatively good pay, before public opinion and inflation began leaning on both.

She taught in places others rejected out of hand, largely because she followed her husband to uranium mines in the Southwest. When he found work in Grants, New Mexico, Audrey left her post in Montezuma County and took a job teaching the children of the miners.

"We didn't have to look at the clock," she told me. "We knew when it was time for lunch because the windows of the school rattled from a regularly scheduled noon-time blast from the mining." The school sat directly atop the mine.

She returned in 1957 to Montezuma County, where she was born, accepted the teacher's job at Battle Rock, moved into the old teacherage, and began her storied run at the school. Occupying the teacherage made her 5:30 A.M. arrivals to the school easier since all she had to do was walk across the Sticker Patch. During the winter months, she went to school even earlier to build fires in the black potbellied stove that sat in the middle of the room. By the time her students arrived, Battle Rock was a warm haven from the frosty winds that whistled through the canyon's corridor and battered the children, some of whom rode to school on horseback.

Reading, writing, and arithmetic were the order of the day, and the basics were blended with the study of nature. When students one year expressed an interest in studying honeybees, Audrey purchased a bee colony from the Montgomery Ward catalogue. She forgot about the order, a thousand bees and their queen, until the mailman delivered a small box that hummed.

"I said to myself, 'Why am I doing this?' Oh, shoot!" she said, laughing at the very idea of setting up a hive at the edge of the Sticker Patch.

Audrey enlisted the assistance of an area beekeeper, and for several seasons the hive produced honey, which students sold at a farmer's market in town. The honey was sold alongside produce from the school garden and the wild asparagus that the children harvested from beside the canyon's several ditches.

Each child had a bank account, and Audrey gave students money based on their work, in and out of the classroom. As a reminder that enterprise paid off, she hung a short poem on one of the school's walls: "Use it up, / Wear it out, / Make it do, / Or do without." When her students faltered, she made them chant the verse in unison. The teacher had a platitude for every occasion.

"We had structure in the class, but within that structure we had freedom and with that freedom came responsibility," she said. Those sentiments, more than any other that came out of Audrey's mouth, were her mantra.

Audrey's fond recollections of Battle Rock belied the gritty and punishing side of life in a canyon. Telephone service was spotty, and the school didn't even have its own line; it shared one with several canyon families. Through most of the twentieth century, McElmo Canyon's residents relied on telephone party lines, and in the year 2000, some portions of Montezuma County still used them. One day, a child broke his arm playing on the Sticker Patch. Audrey rushed to call a doctor. When she picked up the telephone's receiver, a woman known for her verbosity was on the line.

"'Please, this is Battle Rock school, and we have an emergency!'" Audrey remembered telling the woman. "She wanted to know what had happened, and I said 'Please, I need the phone.' She finally cleared the line. Of course, she listened in. Half the time, the phone didn't even work. We were fortunate that day."

Audrey breathed a sigh of relief that day, as she did when a late-winter bus ride into McElmo Canyon from Cortez became anything but routine. A huge boulder, loosened by the melting ice, careened down a hill, and slammed into the crowded school bus. The boulder gave the bus such a whack it was thrown across the road and came to rest along an earthen embankment that met the road. No one was hurt, but the bus's back end was beyond crumpled.

On another occasion, heavy rain washed out a stretch of the road, which occurred with some frequency before it was paved. Audrey sat in the front seat, and when the driver saw a huge swath of the road missing, he braked abruptly. Audrey flew into an airborne somersault and landed in the stairwell near the driver. Workers en route to their jobs at the nearby Aneth Oil Field saw the bus skidding down the canyon road. They worked quickly, stopping their truck and throwing large chains across the road to slow down the bus. The bus stopped a few feet from the edge of the washed-out road. Audrey and the children were shaken and bruised, but no one was seriously injured.

"Oil field workers went down into the canyon with a beer in their hands in the morning and came out in the afternoon with a beer in their hands. They were such trashy old people, but they would always stop if we had trouble with the bus," she said with a tone of true affection in her voice.

Of course, she had her share of discontented parents. Her friendly, melodious voice hardened slightly when she talked about the unappreciative parents that had given her trouble. One year, a woman complained that her child wasn't progressing quickly enough and blamed Audrey for her child's academic mediocrity. Audrey invited the parent to sit with her one school day. The woman watched Audrey start the fire early in the morning, teach all day, make lunch for some of the children, sweep and clean the school, clean the outhouses, and then grade the day's work before she went home. The parent never complained again.

The classroom demands were heavy, but so was watching the children on the Sticker Patch. One year a monstrous badger dug its home beneath the school's stone foundation. Audrey kept a watchful eye on the badger hole when students played.

"It was a big, mean ornery thing," she said. "One day the kids were playing, and the ball rolled into the badger's hole. The big kids found a little kid and lowered him into the hole. I came out, and thought I was going to die! The badger still lived in that hole." The children got their ball, and the young child wasn't hurt.

Sometimes it was the school mascot that posed danger. One year Audrey relented to the children's request for a school pet and ordered a rooster from a catalogue. The children named it Spuds. But the rooster was bad-tempered. "He was meaner than mean," said Audrey. "That rooster was better than a watch dog." The rooster chased and frightened students so much that Audrey finally decided to take him to her home, where the rooster ultimately attacked the wrong person, Audrey's son. "Dave was bending over, and Spuds attacked him on his back with his claws. Dave said, 'That's it,' and went into the house and got his gun and shot Spuds into a million pieces. I couldn't find enough pieces to bury him, so I let the skunks finish him off."

There was always a danger of mountain lions in those days, and the threat prompted Audrey to hide a gun in the file cabinet that stood next to her Army surplus desk. But on one of the very rare occasions she used it, she didn't fire on a mountain lion, or on a menacing badger. She fired on two men.

"A small orphaned fawn had taken up residence in the grape patch next to the schoolhouse," she said. "We adopted and cared for her. One day during the noon hour, the kids were eating their lunches on the old dead tree next to the hayfield where the fawn was grazing, not fifty yards away. A pickup approached from the west. Suddenly two shots rang out, and the fawn, no larger than a collie dog, collapsed, torn to pieces. Two men jumped out of the pickup, leaped the fence, and cut off the fawn's head."

The children screamed at the men, who quickly took the fawn's carcass and sped away. Audrey quickly retrieved the pistol she had in her filing cabinet and, taking aim, fired three shots above the cab of the retreating pickup. The men were gone, but Audrey called gaming officials to report them. It wasn't even hunting season.

"One little girl rushed into the hayfield, and when I reached her, she was sitting on the ground, covered with blood, holding the fawn's head in her lap and crying hysterically."

"Audrey, why did they do this?" the child asked the teacher.

"I didn't have an answer. We cried, all of us, that afternoon," she remembered.

As the years rolled by, the changing sensibilities were not on the school's side. Audrey managed to keep Battle Rock open on three different occasions, but other rural schools weren't so fortunate. Thousands of one-room schools were closed in the first half of the twentieth century, as the construction of the country's ambitious farm-to-market road system made isolated rural communities more accessible to nearby towns. As one-room schools became less remote, they were seen as expensive alternatives to the centrally located school typically found in the county seat or the closest town. Just over 41,000 of these tiny schools were shut down in the 1920s, the highest number of closures of any decade. The massive closings continued through the end of the 1980s, before the 1990s' urban migration fueled the one-room school's modest comeback.

Battle Rock, Audrey told me, was protected for decades by the simple fact that it was remote and sat in a canyon whose terrain made an improved road prohibitively expensive. When the local district again tried to close Battle Rock in the 1970s, Audrey successfully dissuaded officials, arguing that the unpaved canyon road was too treacherous for a school bus, especially in winter. No one knew better than she did.

And so with the passing of the seasons, Audrey settled into life at the school, where she designed a curriculum that eventually won her state-teacher-of-the-year honors. But the past caught up with Audrey when her husband, Lee, died of lung cancer from his years in the uranium mines. A brother, two uncles, and two male cousins, all miners, also succumbed to cancer.

"My husband retired, and we had so many plans. We were going to travel and do all sorts of projects, and nine months after he retired, he was gone," she said quietly. "Lung cancer. Shoot." She received a large lump-sum settlement from the government, money that allowed her to buy the home in which she now lived. In quieter moments with friends, Audrey wondered how soon the U.S. government knew exposure to uranium signed death sentences for the men and women who worked the mines.

"Don't you think they knew from the beginning?" she asked me.

"Probably," I said. "But no one knew asbestos was harmful when it was first used in construction, so who knows?"

Following her husband's death, Audrey funneled even more energy into the school and the Battle Rock 4-H Club, and her affiliation with both transformed the now middle-aged teacher into a local icon. Many of her students now occupied public office or positions in law enforcement or ran businesses, farms, and ranches. Everyone in town recognized her pickup truck, and one afternoon while driving home, she was alarmed when a Cortez police car began following her with its lights swirling and siren blaring. She checked her speed. She pulled over and stopped, and the officer walked up to her truck.

"What did I do wrong?" Audrey asked.

"Oh, nothing, Audrey. I just wanted to say hi," replied the officer. She studied the man and realized he was a former student.

Audrey smiled. She asked about his wife and children, and the
former teacher and former student visited on the roadside, semis
and trailers, pickup trucks, and cars zipping by.

Three hours after arriving for dinner, I bid Audrey a good
night and left for the drive back into town. Audrey had her de-
tractors, to be sure. Some canyon residents had complained to
me about her dated teaching techniques, how she stirred controversy because she sometimes didn't hold her tongue. She did not
suffer fools—that much I gleaned from my visit that night and
during subsequent conversations with her.

Some Cortezians swore she belonged alongside the statue of
Saint Margaret Mary that stood in front of Cortez's single
Catholic church. The tan brick church with an immaculate lawn
stood on Montezuma Avenue, the town's prettiest street. Some local residents declared that Audrey deserved a place next to the
statue of the long-suffering seventeenth-century French nun,
even if she was a Mormon. Which is why what happened to Audrey shocked the good people of Montezuma County.

*L*ike an avalanche, the controversy grew larger and acceler-
ated and then buried everyone in its path. And that's what happened to Audrey in the spring of 1993.

Toward the end of that school year, Audrey decided she
needed an assistant to help with the younger children. She asked
the Cortez school district for an aide; officials said no, the district
couldn't afford the expense this year. Audrey then decided she
could teach the nineteen students the following fall without an
aide. After all, some years she had taught nearly thirty students
at Battle Rock. But the district unilaterally decided to give the
teacher some relief by moving the top three grades to Cortez
schools, shrinking Battle Rock to a K–3 school.

"When this got out, some of the parents thought I had requested that they should be sent to town," Audrey told me when I returned for another visit. "One parent seized the opportunity to pay back a grudge which she had harbored all summer, and one that I knew nothing about. Here was a golden chance to get even. The grudge originated when, on the last day of school the year before, her son had not received a certificate at the awards ceremony. She told other parents I had betrayed them by requesting some of the grades be sent to town."

The district's decision, combined with the woman's story, unsettled McElmo Canyon residents. They began circulating a petition to save the school, but several residents told me it was so poorly written that they thought they were supporting the school, when in fact they had signed a petition asking for Audrey's removal. As canyon residents took the petition door to door, residents were told, if they didn't sign the document, the Cortez school district would close Battle Rock. The momentum overtook any possibility of reason prevailing.

At the same time, Audrey made quiet inquiries into her retirement benefits. Word began circulating in the canyon that Audrey was retiring, when she had no plans to do so. She was sixty-five, and like anyone close to retirement, she had been monitoring her benefits for several years. But in a small town, it seemed, one's business was everyone's business. It was hard to get to the bottom of who passed on sensitive information. No one, of course, owned up to starting idle and, as it happens, inaccurate information that spread through the canyon like wildfire. When I made more inquiries about Audrey's departure, the stories were so varied, or so contradicted each other, that I finally put the most stock in the versions told to me by school district officials and by Audrey herself.

The confusion reached its climax when about fifteen parents presented the petition to the Cortez school board. The board declined to remove the veteran teacher, who was also the school district's highest paid. A school board didn't summarily dismiss a state teacher of the year. Audrey remained at Battle Rock. But after the months of tumult, she quit the week before school began. She marched into the superintendent's office and resigned.

"Send a substitute," she told him. "I can't do this anymore."

As the story came to its entangled end, nearly everyone drew the same conclusion. "It was the worst mistake we ever made in the canyon," said Sheldon Zwicker, who had been taught by Audrey as a boy in the 1950s and who helped circulate the petition that ultimately led to her departure. "I apologized to her."

So did others. Some parents even called school district administrators to say that they had signed the petition in error. As far as Audrey was concerned, the efforts were too late. "They thought I was going behind their backs," she said. "I was so hurt and burned that I couldn't go back."

Montezuma County was incensed. The *Denver Post* covered Audrey's departure, and the local paper declared the veteran teacher should have received more consideration. "Audrey deserved better after 48 years," the *Cortez Journal* wrote in an editorial. That much is certain.

"She put a lot more in the school than she ever got back," Stephen Hanson said one day. Audrey herself knew what Stephen had gone through and sympathized with her successor. The two teachers were linked beyond their acquaintanceship by adversity.

Seven years after the petition drive toppled her, Audrey rarely ventured much into the depths of the canyon, and not since her retirement had she stepped foot in Battle Rock. There were too many memories—the recent ones bad—and she knew few of the children.

"So much has changed down there," she lamented one day. "I don't know anyone down there, seems like, anymore. So many of the kids at the school are from town. And I don't know about this charter school business. Maybe they will make it. I hope they make it."

*O*n a *cool winter night* a steady stream of pickup trucks full of children began arriving at a small, boxlike building near Audrey's house. This was, of course, the clubhouse advertised in the short item I had read in the *Journal* a week earlier. The building was actually an eighty-four-year-old former one-room school in which Audrey herself had attended fourth through sixth grades. When the school district put the old building up for sale, her son purchased it for $200 and, with help from friends, moved it from its location about a mile away to Audrey's place. A 4-H parent wired the building for electricity, and Audrey still used the old wood-burning stove that had warmed her as a girl in the school.

The old schoolhouse found another life as the bustling headquarters for the Battle Rock 4-H Club, the oldest, most decorated, and as it happened, the richest of Montezuma County's twelve chapters. Seventy children from the canyon and other communities across Montezuma County were members, and sometimes the spacious clubhouse barely had enough chairs to accommodate the assembled throng. I arrived early and was immediately drawn to several colorful posters. They featured thirty-two different breeds of chickens, some of them laying colored eggs, some of them just for show—pretty multicolored roosters and hens whose single purpose in life was to strut in all their glory in someone's front yard. I figured they were rural America's answer to the plastic pink flamingos that adorned some urban front yards.

One by one, children entered the clubhouse with their parents in tow. By the time the meeting started, there were nearly fifty people in the room, along with a box of rabbits one family brought to sell. I looked over the back of the chair in front of me and peered into the box. It was difficult to tell where one bunny stopped and another began.

"Do you want to buy one?" the woman asked. "Only ten dollars."

"No, thanks," I said.

"They make great pets," she said.

"I'm sure," I replied.

Before she could continue her sales pitch, Audrey called the meeting to order. She recalled the club members' triumphs at the previous summer's Montezuma County Fair, which had been particularly good to the Battle Rock 4-H Club. Members had won grand champion and reserve champion honors for sheep, rabbits, and other livestock, and each child now received rousing applause from smiling parents as they retrieved their blue and red ribbons. After the meeting, parents and children lingered to eat a chili supper and nibble on cookies Audrey made from scratch.

She still sometimes yearned for Battle Rock, wistful for another run at the school. Looking back on a half century of teaching, she shook her head at how ideas and notions of learning took on cycles. In her day, it was peer learning; today, it was mutually aided learning. In her day, it was citizenship class; today, civic or community service. It was all one and the same, she thought, and then, as now, parents and the public complained about teachers and all the things that schools did wrong.

"Oh, shit!" she said, laughing at the ridiculousness of it all. Sometimes even a good Mormon woman had to let loose because "Oh, shoot" didn't quite do it.

Chapter 14

Faith, and a Miracle

*O*n *most days,* Kayla stayed indoors at lunch, content to quietly eat alone, read, or visit with her younger classmates. Her ruptured friendship with Debbie and Connie never improved in the months following the letter she gave to the two girls. On occasion I joined her with the lunch I had purchased that morning from the Texaco Amigo Mart. One day, however, she skipped lunch entirely. She sipped on hot tea as she pensively walked around the room. A second grader asked Kayla what was wrong before I could.

"Why aren't you eating?" he asked.

Stephen overhead the question and asked Kayla if she was ill. Teresa and I looked up from our lunches to hear the reply.

"No. I'm fasting," Kayla said.

"Why?" Stephen asked.

"My pastor's wife had an aneurysm."

"I'm sorry," Stephen said.

"My mom and I are fasting."

Kayla told Stephen, Teresa, and her inquisitive classmate that her fast began right after breakfast and ended right before dinner, so she only missed lunch. She pursued her fast with an understatement that the teacher had grown to expect from and admire in the eleven-year-old. "She didn't make a big deal of it and boast. She just did it," Stephen later remarked to Teresa, who nodded in agreement.

For the next two weeks, with quiet purpose, Kayla skipped lunch on behalf of one Dolly Henderson, who lay comatose in a hospital bed in Grand Junction, two hundred miles north of Cortez. The minister's wife had suffered a stroke on January 15 and was flown four days later to Grand Junction's larger and better-equipped hospital. By the time the Reverend Don Henderson and his wife landed in Grand Junction, Dolly had slipped into a coma, a state in which she languished for more than a month. Nearly two hundred cards and countless bouquets of flowers arrived at Dolly's hospital room, many of them from members of the First Assembly Church of God and other well-wishers back home in Cortez, where the town's faithful fasted and prayed for her recovery—in short, for a miracle.

One Sunday morning shortly after Kayla had started her fast, I joined her and the rest of the Burns family at church. I parked my Jeep and observed the people walking through the doors of the simply constructed tan brick building. Most of the people were longtime Cortezians who were, on the whole, simple, proud, and decent people. But the church also counted among its members a growing number of urban families like the Burnses. A large cross constructed of thick wood beams hung over the church's double front door. Inside, the varnished pews were set off by deep red carpet. As the service began, Brenda Burns leaned over to me and whispered, "We kind of rock here."

Rock the church did. There was a full hour of soul-rousing singing striking themes of love and salvation. A small choir, a pianist, an organist, a French horn, guitar, and drums accompanied the congregation's collection of clear, strong voices. The music was followed by an hour-long sermon by Rev. Henderson, who had returned that weekend from visiting his wife in Grand Junction.

Forgiveness was the theme. In a direct, no-nonsense message, the minister's sermon struck a chord with me; during the opening minutes I decided his advice had many more practical applications than taking the high road with people, a noble pursuit in itself. The minister didn't specifically address the role forgiveness played in rural communities, but some residents had already talked to me about the importance of taking a long view of people and relationships in a small place. In communities where everyone knew each other—if not personally, then by name and reputation—residents told me they had to learn to turn the other cheek, especially in the aftermath of a disagreement. Those who didn't or couldn't forgive a transgression, I observed, led lonely lives. There was also the matter of awkward meetings at the post office or grocery store or on Main Street. In cities, you could fade into a sea of humanity, but in a small town, people were forced to face each other far more often.

As the minister continued his appeal, I was reminded of another fundamental reason for cultivating a life around a church. I thought back to a lunch I had had a few weeks earlier with one of the town's Baptist ministers and remembered a seemingly mundane conversation about my refrigerator. When the one in my rented house broke down, I called a repairman listed in the phone book on three different occasions and left messages each time on his answering machine. Finally on the fourth call, his wife picked up the phone. I explained who I was and told her my problem.

"Haven't you received my calls?" I asked.

"Yes, I heard them," the wife said. "My husband doesn't like answering machines, so he doesn't answer them. But he did hear your messages when I played them. He'll come by."

"When?" I asked.

"Soon," came the reply. "Call this evening. He'll be here."

The man finally did come to my house and looked at why the refrigerator froze my food and the freezer didn't. He said he would come back with a part and then never returned. I didn't even bother to call again, instead defrosting the refrigerator every three weeks, which seemed to correct the problem. It was the first of many such experiences, and I wondered how business people, this one in particular, made money providing such unreliable service.

When I shared my refrigerator story with the minister, he told me, "Oh, I wish I had known. We have a church member who does that kind of work. We have a plumber too. In the future if you have need of either, call the church office, and we'll see that you're moved to the top of the list."

"So, this is how it works here?" I asked.

"Yes," the minister replied. "We don't have an electrician, but maybe someone will join the church soon."

Many urban people new to Montezuma County didn't come to this particular lesson very quickly, and most urbanites I encountered did not attend church regularly. So they didn't get food for the soul, and their dripping faucets or broken refrigerators weren't repaired very quickly.

As Rev. Henderson completed his sermon, I stood with the rest of the congregation for the final prayer. As he prayed, people in the pews raised their hands and faces heavenward, punctuating the minister's words with "Yes, Lord!" and "Amen!" and "Yes, Jesus!"

I *would be stretching the truth* to say I reclaimed my spirituality in Cortez, but my year in the town forced me to examine my life. Nearly two decades of urban living in New York, San Francisco, and Dallas had produced a lifestyle that needed reevaluation and, ultimately, aggressive pruning. Living in a rural community with life's volume turned down eventually produced a stripped-down version of my previous life. I had no choice really. There were far fewer amenities and distractions in a small town. But much of my self-improvement campaign was intentional. This exercise, imposed on me by the quietness of a small town, began on a warm summer night at the end of my first week in Cortez.

On a Sunday evening in August of 1999, when residents of Cortez were taking in the final days of a golden summer, I joined a group of people gathered at the First Assembly church for a prayer meeting. This was no typical church gathering. Nearly five months after the worst school shooting spree in U.S. history left thirteen people dead at Columbine High School in suburban Denver, Cortez's God-fearing, church-going residents decided their schools needed stronger protections than the state's gun control laws, a barrage of legislation that had failed Columbine. One by one, they showed up at the church—members of Baptist, Methodist, Church of Christ, and Assembly of God congregations—everyone, it seemed, who had heard the call from their pulpits that Sunday morning. Many Cortezians were churchgoers, and they prayed for and about everything. They prayed for rain for crops; they prayed for successful harvests and healthy livestock. Why not for safe schools?

I arrived at the First Assembly that night for the first time and counted close to one hundred people as they walked through the doors to pray for teachers and staff, for students and their families. When they finished, they took their prayers to the schools themselves. In groups of two or more, they walked or drove to the schools to petition the Lord for divine protection in a world that had rendered many schools killing grounds in the last years of the twentieth century.

I followed one man, Merlin Elliott, on his appointment with God. He drove his bright-blue van into the depths of McElmo Canyon and pulled into the gravel lot of Battle Rock, where his two granddaughters were scheduled to begin school the following morning. "After what happened up there at Columbine, our schools need prayer," he told me, as we quietly walked around the deserted Sticker Patch that warm night. "I don't think gun control will do any good, but prayer always helps." He quietly prayed for guardian angels to watch over Battle Rock, Stephen, and his twenty-six students.

In the months that followed, I noticed manifestations of the town's enduring and very visible faith. Every morning on my way to the canyon from my rented flat in Cortez, I drove by the M&M truck stop. Not only could a traveler get sustenance from a full menu, but the truck stop also supplied a small chapel, painted in baby blue, in a corner of its parking lot. Services were announced on the restaurant's intercom system, and the chapel, which accommodated no more than a dozen people, often drew a standing-room-only crowd. Truckers, and presumably any other traveler, could also marry at the chapel if love struck them while they were on the road. Not to be outdone, the Hunan Chinese Restaurant at the other end of town played Christian hymns at lunch, and at Christmas, diners were treated to hymns in Chinese.

Newcomers looking for a church home had only to read the *Cortez Journal* every Saturday. The newspaper's church directory consumed a full page and boasted sixty-five listings, an astonishingly high number for a town of 8,000 people. There was the Bethel Baptist Church ("Where People Come to Life"), the Church of Christ ("Where You're Always Welcome"), New Hope Christian Fellowship ("A 'down home' Pentecostal church where God is moving") and the proud-to-be-informal Rico Community Presbyterian Church ("Fishermen, hunters, mountain climbers, miners, all others—come as you are"). The town's handful of Jewish families had to travel to Durango for the nearest synagogue, and the Catholics had St. Margaret Mary. The First Assembly of God, at seventy members, was one of the town's largest.

The zealousness startled some urban people new to Montezuma County, but surveys and polls had long shown that rural people are more devout than urban Americans and are twice as likely to talk about religion at work than city dwellers. In fact, I first heard about Dolly's recovery not from Kayla and not from the pulpit at the First Assembly of God. A clerk at an office supply store in downtown Cortez told me. She sang in the First Assembly choir.

"Isn't God great?" she asked me after telling me the news.

"Yes, He is," I replied.

I heard the full details later that week from Kayla, who shared the news with Stephen and her Battle Rock classmates at lunch. Kayla told us with wide eyes that Dolly emerged from her coma on her birthday. Dolly recuperated a few more days in Grand Junction and then returned to Cortez, where she attended her first Sunday service in months. Visibly weaker and a bit pale but standing with the help of a cane, she was inundated with good wishes and welcomes from her church family. As far as the Burnses and other members of First Assembly of God were concerned, there was no equivocation. God, they believed, had delivered a miracle.

A few weeks after Dolly returned to Cortez, I paid Rev. Henderson a visit at his home to talk about this miracle, about life in a small town, and about his take on Montezuma County's growth. I drove down Main Street and turned near the McDonald's, one of the many fast-food franchises built in recent years to accommodate the town's growth. The Hendersons lived at the end of a tree-lined street in a pretty frame house with a large shade tree. As the minister sat in a comfortable chair in his living room, he recounted his wife's illness and recovery that had tested his faith.

"God had a hand in all of this," he told me. "Doctors never used the word *miracle,* but they weren't optimistic, either. Doctors said she was as close to death as she could be and still be alive. Was it a miracle? I have heard people say that, but I don't know. The medical community was involved. She is still in speech therapy and will be for some time. In many ways, I guess you could say it was a miracle."

As if on cue, Dolly walked into the living room and greeted me and then returned to her bedroom for rest. We settled in for a long visit. Did the minister think rural communities were more devout? I asked.

"Historically, I think this has been true," he said. "The Bible has recorded it. The rural people were more dedicated to their faith. It comes down to priorities and time consumption and lifestyle. You go into your cities, and it's frightening to me.

"In cities, success to your metropolitan people means position and possessions," he continued. "In rural areas, relationships are far more important—relationships and religion. A relationship with God. You have to have time to smell the flowers, too, and see the stars. Here, it's the mountains. You'll hear people say they feel closer to God in the mountains or in the woods. And there is a reason for that. If you are out and there are no television sets, no newspapers, fewer people, you have less distractions. God reveals himself in his handiwork, and that is biblical.

"People have come back to rural America because of what the place offers," he said. "God called me here for this time, and this is where I belong right now."

Except for the years he spent at a Seattle seminary, he had spent his entire career in small towns. His first congregation took him to rural Kansas, then to Sterling, Colorado, a rural community north of Denver. In 1993, he moved to Cortez, where he continued to enjoy the pace of a rural life, what that life offered, and just as important, what it didn't. "I know of only one place, south of town, that has pornography," he told me. "In cities it's on the street corners."

The minister didn't especially like how outside pressures were bearing down on Montezuma County's communities. In the mid-1990s, rumors circulated that West Coast gangs were moving to Cortez, and Rev. Henderson, who also served as a chaplain to the town's law enforcement agencies, had the inside scoop. As the story went, the young men were required to steal to be initiated into the gang. They broke into First Assembly of God, found the petty cash box, and stole the money. At another church, they defecated on the altar and then tore pages from the Bible to use as toilet paper.

The threat of hard-core gangs never materialized in Cortez, and the rampage of guns in schools both urban and rural never reached Cortez. For that the Reverend Henderson was thankful, as he was for Battle Rock.

The minister considered the one-room school a unique place because it allowed both Kayla and her younger brother, Shane, to express their faith without derision from the other children. He attributed the school's tolerant environment to Stephen. In the fall, for example, Shane had written a school essay on creationism, its teaching so controversial that it was beaten out of most public school curricula over the years, if it had even been allowed at all. Stephen simply offered tips on how to improve Shane's creationism essay, then graded it and posted it on the bulletin board that displayed other student reports that month. Though the teacher eschewed prayer around the school flagpole and posting the Ten Commandments in the school—both issues that regularly confront courts across the nation—Stephen gave his students expansive freedom to express themselves in their essays. In their teacher, Kayla and Shane had a quiet champion. Stephen himself regularly attended Saturday night mass with Susan at St. Margaret Mary Catholic Church.

Chapter 15

Living on the Edge

The noisy screen door at G Whil Liquors slammed closed as another customer walked into the store's air-conditioned confines.

"Hi, there!" Teresa Blakney said. "We have beer on sale today." The customer smiled and looked for something harder.

I sat behind the counter sipping a Diet Pepsi and, between the screen door's squeaky openings and closings, watched Teresa work her sales and bookkeeping job at the liquor store that sat at the western edge of Cortez. The position was the latest in a string of jobs Teresa had held in the three years since she returned from Phoenix. Following her sister's advice "to lower your expectations, you're moving to Cortez," Teresa had continually adjusted her expectations downward. Her job at Battle Rock as Stephen's aide helped generate some income, but for several months during the school year she was often looking for more work, or quitting one job that was low paying to find another job that paid only slightly more. In one of these stretches, she used her local ties to find G Whil Liquors's position, a far cry from the office manager's position she held for a Phoenix doctor. "I'm embarrassed to be working here," she told me that afternoon. "If I could find another job, I would."

The store sometimes generated more than $1,000 in a day. Not that Teresa saw much of it. She earned between $200 and $300 every two weeks, despite performing several tasks. She balanced the books, cleaned the store, and stocked the shelves and refrigerators with boxes of liquor. One day she sprained her hand from all the lifting. She put a brace on her hand and kept working. She had no choice.

She finally quit the liquor store in April and took a position she felt was even more degrading, so she told no one. She found work cleaning rooms at a local motel that served the tourist traffic, and in stretches, worked harder there than peddling liquor. She had twenty minutes to make the beds, clean the bathroom, and dust and vacuum. Her sprained hand hurt even more. The motel's management was punitive. "One day, they called us all in and told us we were lucky to have jobs with them because we were easily replaced," Teresa remembers. "They talked to us like we were idiots."

Teresa decided she was no idiot. Soon after that meeting, she decided the motel could operate without her services. She left the position a few weeks later, beginning the process again of finding work in a town where, she discovered, the best jobs always seemed to be taken by inside candidates. I watched the Blakneys with amazement. For all their underemployment and, in long stretches, their unemployment, they never seemed to go hungry. They were always well dressed. Their home was well furnished, and Teresa's vintage doll collection was displayed in a handsome oak cabinet. How did they manage?

*M*any *Cortezians,* truth be told, lived on the slightest of incomes. Several Battle Rock parents found work out of town or were underemployed or unemployed if they stayed in town. One girl's parents followed construction work across the state with the highway department. The child lived with her grandmother. Another father worked a string of part-time jobs, none of which ever paid a gainful wage. Another parent worked at McDonald's. Out of necessity, a good number of Cortezians turned squeezing a penny into an art.

The frustrations bubbled to the surface when Governor Bill Owens came calling one afternoon to generate support for expansion of the state's Interstate 25 corridor. The interstate's urban stretch ran from Fort Collins in the north, through Denver, to Colorado Springs in the south, a distance of 130 miles. Colorado's booming economy had attracted several hundred thousand new residents to the state in the 1990s, and the interstate showed it with rush-hour traffic approaching Los Angeles–like proportions. After the governor made his pitch at the Anasazi Motor Inn Convention Center, locals wondered aloud how improving Denver's traffic flow was of any help to Montezuma County. The governor wasn't going to get off easy. Not in Cortez.

"So you want Denver to be so unpleasant that people would move out here?" the governor asked, smiling.

The exchange was civil, and manners were minded. But Cortezians were in no mood to be nickeled-and-dimed. Local employers did that well enough. The governor's very presence was occasion for remarks.

"This has nothing to do with what we're talking about, really, but why is it the only time we see our state officials out here is when you people are running for office or you want something?" asked a white-haired lady. She was, in fact, correct. Few state officials bothered with communities on the Western Slope, the land that lay to the west of the Rocky Mountains.

"We'll try to do better," the governor promised.

The governor was soon gone, but he didn't have to wait long for his reviews. A month later, when Colorado voters considered the interstate bond issue, Montezuma County was the only one of the state's sixty-three counties to reject the project.

Cortez had economic potential, but like the gold and silver deposits that eluded the early settlers, that promise wasn't easily mined. The town's remoteness, one of its biggest problems, was compounded by a simple problem: getting in and out of the place was only nominally easier in the 1990s than decades before. At the end of the twentieth century, the town still had no regular bus service, it still suffered from the absence of rail connections, and for a time, air service was so irregular that it was virtually useless. Flights were canceled constantly, with little or no notice, stranding Cortezians at Denver International Airport. Sometimes when the airline actually flew, residents wondered why it even bothered. One Cortez businesswoman remembers flying back to Montezuma County after a day of meetings in Denver and watching in horror as the pilot completely overshot the single runway at Cortez Municipal Airport. The second attempt at landing was successful, and the woman recalls passengers were shaking their heads in disbelief and disgust as they disembarked.

The situation became so intolerable that the *Cortez Journal* finally ran a lengthy front-page article in the fall of 1999 documenting the air service's late arrivals and failures to arrive at all. The paper then decried the airline's shoddiness in an editorial, pointing out—in case anyone missed the relationship—that reliable air travel was key to economic development.

As air service improved, so did the community's job recruitment efforts. But even here, the town was forced to exercise care in the type of company it recruited, because its infrastructure was outdated, or overburdened, or both. Cortez's wastewater treatment plant had labored mightily over the years as a result of the town's 1990s population boom. When City Manager Hal Shepherd arrived from Hamilton, Ohio, where he had held a similar post, he was stunned to discover no provisions had been made to build a new one.

"Nobody operates at capacity," he said, shaking his head in disbelief. "When I asked the head of the agency that manages the treatment plant about this and I told him he had to prepare for growth, he told me, 'Well, just because other counties are growing doesn't mean we will.'" The city manager gave me a look that I had come to recognize. It was the same reaction of utter astonishment that I had seen on the faces of other newcomers who, through a variety of experiences, realized the town was a monumental work in progress. Even if the town had succeeded in luring more jobs, officials had to be prudent about the number of positions and the type of industry it attracted. The wastewater treatment plant could accommodate only four hundred more jobs, they figured, and only if they were light industry or service sector positions that didn't produce a lot of waste.

These weren't the only issues the town faced, but I didn't need officials to tell me about the next hurdle. In the year I lived there, telecommunication service was so poor that in long stretches my email through Farmers Online Network, or fone.net, did not work. Sometimes the electricity and phone went out in my old rented farmhouse in the middle of a sunny, cloudless day. The first time it happened, I found my landlord working his yard and asked him about the blackout. It's not as if Cortez powered hundreds of street lights and traffic signals. Sometimes high winds and punishing winter storms downed the lines, he said. But the truth had less to do with nature.

"We live in a crappy service area," he told me.

He didn't get an argument from me.

The dismal state of the local job market ranked high on the typical Cortezian's list of complaints, right after the grumbling about outsiders. I heard their laments in barbershops, in conversations at the grocery store, in lines at the post office. But in a contradiction lost on most, locals didn't want the higher taxes for a new treatment plant or other projects. In truth, many could not have afforded to pay higher taxes of any kind given the thinness of the job market. Then there were the Cortezians who wanted better employment opportunities and were quite prepared to pay for them; but there was a condition.

"We want more and better paying jobs here, but for our people," a county official told me one afternoon. "Jobs for local people, not outsiders." She told me that outsiders were ruining Cortez, that urban people, especially Californians, were rude or arrogant or both. I couldn't argue with her take on some of the new city people who had moved to the county. I too had overheard their condescending remarks in the stores and had seen them patronize the local people working sales jobs and other service positions.

But some of these new neighbors, I told her, had business skills that could help lift Cortez out of its economic malaise. She shot me a surprised look, quickly followed by one of disdain. In that moment, I realized I had committed heresy for suggesting, God forbid, that urban people could actually prove beneficial to the town. Her looks also reminded me that I was the embodiment of everything locals detested: I was an outsider who generated more traffic. I had the exceedingly bad judgment to be a liberal Democrat. Worse, I had actually lived earlier in my life in California, a den of iniquity where everyone was on drugs and disrespected America. So went the local tirade. When I left her office in the Montezuma County Courthouse, I concluded that without some major adjustments in attitude the place would languish for another century. Cortez, very simply, often cut its own throat.

Locals didn't want to hear or acknowledge that they were forty-seven miles west of a successful economic development case study. Durango had a vibrant tourist trade, with its historic narrow-gauge steam-powered train rumbling into town, blowing thick plumes of smoke along the edge of the picturesque mountain community. Durango had countless shops that sold handmade jewelry and a rich selection of Native American blankets and pottery. The town boasted inviting bookstores and art galleries, fine dining, and a beautifully restored turn-of-the-century hotel. Most importantly, the town had jobs.

Durango, overrun years ago by the urban people Cortezians loathed, heralded itself as the "Gateway to Mesa Verde," the national park that is home to the Anasazi cliff dwellings, billed in 1999 by the National Geographic Society as the world's second most popular tourist destination, after India's magical Taj Mahal. Durango's claim rightfully belonged to Cortez. The mesa that protected the extensive ruins was in Montezuma County and visible from many places in town.

Savvy Cortezian businessmen and -women—and there were many in town—were well aware how badly the town and county scored when compared to other small communities like Durango. Yet Cortez failed to capitalize fully on its unique location or follow the marketing leads of other small hamlets, which for decades had concocted festivals and fairs built around historic events and places, or promoted fruit, vegetables, or flowers to lure visitors. But Cortez didn't have anything remotely comparable. The reason, I was told by more than one person, was simple: so many people in town worked long hours at two, sometimes three, jobs to make ends meet. As a result, there was little time to organize a festival or fair and then see it through. No one wanted Cortez to become another Durango, and many residents were actually quite happy not to have their town overrun with more people.

Slowly, however, the stubborn attitudes were giving way. By the end of my year in Cortez, a new waste treatment plant was on the drawing board. The town was included in a high-powered telecommunications loop being built in the region. The county economic development board hired a new director, a former NASA engineer, and had $400,000 to spend on getting the word out about "The Friendliest Town in the West." The governor even made good on his promise. In the spring the state attorney general came through town to discuss gun-control efforts in schools. But at a time when many rural communities successfully lurched forward into the twenty-first century, Cortez was off to a very slow start.

*O*ne night the Blakneys invited me to their mobile home for dinner. I drove to the western edge of town, past G Whil Liquors, past the turnoff to McElmo Canyon, and then turned right off the highway that led to Shiprock. I drove down a bumpy gravel road that became an impassable sea of mud after a heavy rain. One year, a resident had placed large rocks and small boulders in the road. The patchwork paving job made the road even bumpier, wet or dry.

When I arrived at the Blakneys' home, Teresa was dicing lettuce and tomatoes and cooking ground beef for Navajo tacos. She had even made the bread from scratch, shaping the dough into circles and deep frying them. We sat down to dinner, and she told me the tomatoes came from her sister's vegetable garden. The dough was on sale. And it occurred to me that Teresa was an inveterate bargain hunter. She shopped at the local dollar store, clipped coupons, and helped plant the vegetable garden at her sister's home a few miles away. The garden kept the Blakneys, her sister's family, and their mother in fresh produce during the growing season. This, then, was how they managed.

Teresa drew the line, however, at roadkill. "You know," she told me, "the Colorado State Patrol maintains a list, and when a deer or elk is killed, the name at the top of the list is called, and they have to go out quickly and get the carcass. You can call, and they'll put your name on the list."

This was news to me. Several of their friends, she said, had dined on venison and elk, compliments of a driver who mowed down an animal that had bad timing. The Blakneys themselves had been the recipient of meat harvested by a motorist. They might have had more venison one year if Teresa had actually struck the deer that darted out in front of her Jeep.

"I swerved one way, then another way, and I missed the deer," she said, laughing, as we drank our coffee in their living room. "I don't know how I avoiding hitting it. Everything moved so fast. When I told my mom, she scolded me for not hitting it. We could have had some venison, she said. But then I thought the damage to my car would have been more than the meat was worth."

In the months that followed, I noticed their efforts began paying off. Bill became an assistant manager at a local pizza restaurant in November 2000, and three months later, he created a limited partnership through which he bought the franchise, but not the ovens and other hardware, from the owner in nearby Dolores. Bill hired four employees, most of whom delivered the pizzas, and operated his restaurant on a strictly cash basis.

"It's easier that way," he said one night, spreading sauce on dough that Teresa had made earlier in the evening. "Right now the restaurant is paying the bills for the food, and it's paying my bills."

Pizza Pockets generated a brisk business, even during the slow winter months, when tourists didn't visit Mesa Verde National Park. On those frenetic winter nights, Bill and Teresa moved even faster, with Teresa kneading extra dough for orders that were phoned in. The busiest nights hurt her hand, a reminder of the sprain she suffered at the liquor store and exacerbated by making beds at the motel. Bill had his own wounds. Both of his arms were covered with burns that marked the numerous times he had brushed up against the industrial-sized oven as he retrieved the bubbling pizzas. But owning a pizza business was better than working highway construction, or working at a liquor store or motel.

The store earned between $200 and $250 a day during the slow winter months, enough to pay the store's and the couple's bills. During the school year, Stephen had promoted Teresa to full-time status, and the family began to inch its way back to financial stability. They wondered, like a lot of other people, whether Cortez would ever do the same.

Chapter 16

"How Well Are We Doing?"

A few weeks after returning from his Crestone teachers' meeting, Stephen assembled the school's third and fourth graders in the teacherage for a rite of passage. The six students, evenly distributed between the two grades, were scheduled to take Colorado's standardized exam that gauged students' progress in reading, writing, and critical-thinking skills. Although Battle Rock's charter school status allowed it to operate independently from the Montezuma-Cortez School District, the teacher was still required to administer the Colorado Standardized Assessment Program, or CSAP. As Stephen's students took their seats in the teacherage, he knew the two-day exam was also a measure of his teaching skills.

The test required students to read short stories and answer several comprehension questions—some multiple-choice and some written short response—on each. Other exercises in-structed them to read a vignette, write short, written responses, and then correct spelling, punctuation, and grammatical errors. The test scores were the subject of teacher-parent conferences, front-page newspaper stories, and editorials praising or decrying the results depending on whether scores increased or declined from the year before. Battle Rock was coming off a stellar year. The previous year, the children had scored a 100 percent profi-ciency on the exam and won the school a state honor for excel-lence. Stephen wondered whether they could do it again.

"How long are we going to be doing this?" asked one of the third graders.

"For two days," he answered. "You'll like it. It's fun."

Stephen told the children to write their names and the name of the school in the blanks and then fill in the corresponding bub-bles. The teacherage was still except for the rustle of paper.

"And spell the name of the school correctly, for goodness' sake," the teacher said.

"I don't got a middle name," one boy said.

"You don't *have* a middle name," said Stephen.

Stephen kept reading the instructions, and then he stopped. He gazed at one girl who was disengaged.

"You listening to me?" Stephen asked the girl.

"Uh-huh," she said as she tied her shoe.

Stephen guided the students through several sample exercises before they began the exam.

"Do sample B," he told the students. Stephen now intently watched the third-grade girl who had finished tying her shoe but now sat nearly lifeless at the table. "Do sample B," Stephen told her. "Maybe you stayed up too late?"

The child did appear groggy and not the least bit prepared for a test of such magnitude. As she worked on the sample exercise, Stephen looked over her shoulder. He winced as the girl pro-duced the wrong answer on the vocabulary question.

"Think. This test requires you to *think,"* said Stephen. After he guided them through the sample questions, the children started the exam. Stephen quietly walked around the room, reading over their shoulders for his early returns.

"Keep moving, or you won't finish your work," Stephen told one student staring out a window.

As he inspected their work, Stephen didn't like what he saw. "They're blowing it left and right," he said, quietly mouthing the words. "There goes our 100 percent proficiency."

In a tiny school like Battle Rock, when there were only six students in two grades taking the exam, one poor score profoundly skewed the school's average. Three unsatisfactory results were ruinous. Two of the three children producing poor work were new students at Battle Rock this school year, and the third child had enrolled just weeks before the exam. The other students had attended Battle Rock since kindergarten and, under Stephen's constant push to read and write, were doing well on the exam.

Tim was one of the successful students. The boy worked quietly and quickly as he took the exam. He was a voracious reader, and during the afternoons when Stephen allowed the children to read a book at their tables, Tim had read nearly twenty titles by the middle of the spring term and then passed a reading comprehension exam. His thin arms surrounded his paper as he read the short stories.

The hour went quickly, and the teacher collected the work and put it away. Concerned about the first day's showing, Stephen also took a calculated view of the exam.

"I don't care what they do on these tests," he told me after the students had returned to the school for lunch. "I can show that I didn't have them last year, and I didn't get to train them."

*C*olorado *teachers called the exam "C-CRAP."* Teachers here and elsewhere chafed under the mounting testing demands of the 1990s, but they had little choice. If schools asked for more money to improve instruction—and in the last decade many did—state lawmakers argued that schools had to justify the extra money by showing improvement. Tests were the easiest and most efficient way to gauge achievement. But issues surrounding testing, student progress, and a teacher's skills weren't easily addressed or adequately measured by a two-day test. Or so teachers felt.

There were long-standing complaints about bias in tests that, some research concluded, undermined girls and minority students because these exams assumed a body of knowledge that inner-city youngsters, for example, didn't possess. And in rural communities like Cortez, some parents asserted the CSAP discriminated against rural students, because the test assumed knowledge only an urban child could know. There was some truth about how the exams were biased against girls and minority children, and in the 1990s test makers produced more sophisticated exams that placated, but didn't completely satisfy, the critics. The rural charges, however, were so new in the 1990s that little definitive research supported those claims, and in fact, Battle Rock's performance suggested otherwise.

The previous year, Battle Rock's third and fourth graders, most of whom had never lived in an urban area and were poor by federal standards, did so well on the test that the school was one of only 119 to apply for a competitive state award for excellence. This year, half of the six students sitting for the exam lived at or near the poverty level, and most had never lived in a city. But Stephen wasn't so sure these students would do as well as the students did a year ago because several of them were new to the school.

The students who stumbled on the first day of the exam didn't improve on the second day. Although test results weren't available for months, Stephen knew the school wouldn't repeat last year's 100 percent proficiency or earn a state citation for excellence. Not that it mattered. The teacher often thought parents and the public put too much weight on standardized exams. For Stephen, the tests simply provided a snapshot on a continuum of a student's progress. Nothing more.

A month after the students sat for the state exam, Stephen cleared his calendar for parent conferences. The meetings were opportunities for the teacher to talk with parents about their child's progress and what the school and parents could do to help the child improve. These meetings, however, were often heavy lifting. "All through the year," the teacher said, "parents come in and say hello and gloss over the issues, and two times a year we have to deal with the dirt."

Kim Lindgren didn't wait for the parent conferences to air her concerns. In the months since she had been elected to Battle Rock's school board, she offered numerous suggestions on how to bolster what she felt was a weak curriculum. She was vocal about her concerns but grew increasingly unhappy with the teacher's slow response. She wrote him a letter calling him unsupportive.

When Kim arrived at the school, Stephen did not expect an easy time. Eric, who had driven in from Albuquerque for the long weekend, accompanied his wife. Kim repeated her concerns about the school's curriculum.

"What do you want me to do?" Stephen asked them point blank. "What do you want the school to do? I hired Anne because of your concerns." Stephen told the Lindgrens they expected lightning-speed change in the school. "It doesn't happen like that," Stephen said.

No one knew better than the teacher how change in the school had to be introduced carefully, not rashly or quickly. Not after he was fired and rehired. Not after the Botticelli mess. Not after the dozens of other complaints from parents who, he felt, expected him to perform miracles without help from the home. Stephen was prudent about the changes he introduced at Battle Rock.

Stephen's slowness was interpreted a variety of ways by the school community: some parents were content with the school. Others, like Kim, wanted improvements introduced more quickly.

Several weeks after the conference with Stephen, Kim still felt bruised over the brusque way she felt the teacher had spoken to her, as well as over the spreading community buzz that she had targeted the teacher's job. "Everyone thinks this is about Stephen," she said in the living room of her home. "It isn't. It's about getting the best for my daughters." Kim lost sleep, waking up in the middle of the night and getting upset all over again as she replayed the conversation with Stephen. "I sat back a whole year and watched how things worked before I got vocal," she said. "I didn't want to bring my city values here."

When she finally discussed how Battle Rock could offer so much more to its students, Kim got the distinct feeling that other school board members and canyon residents weren't much interested in what she had to say. When Kim approached the school's Accountability Committee with the changes she thought would make the school better, her suggestions were summarily rejected. The Accountability Committee, the school's parental advising arm, was chaired by Teresa, Stephen's assistant.

"Some people sense you are about to make changes, and before you can get your words out, the 'no' comes back," Kim said months into her efforts to improve the school.

The discord had an effect on the teacher too. The behind-the-scenes disagreements made Stephen increasingly quiet, almost remote, in the spring term. Teresa worried about him. She knew something was afoot, though he didn't even tell her, a trusted aide, what was unfolding.

The teacher quietly concluded that he had ceded too much control of the curriculum and teaching to two of his part-time teachers, Anne Wright and another woman, who taught the school's eight first graders, by far Battle Rock's largest class. Stephen had become more of an administrator, a transition necessary to handle the school's budget and bank account, equipment orders, and his involvement in the Colorado Rural Charter School Network. Stephen began to think that, perhaps, he should tighten the reins of the school.

"I told Susan it would be a lot easier if I took over all the teaching again," he said one day after his students had gone home. "It would mean a lot more work for me, but I could maintain some quality control. That way I know what the kids know."

There was an irony in the conflict between Stephen and Kim. Charter schools were intended to pull parents back into the school, make them active participants in their child's education. Parental and community participation looked good on paper, but in practice, with so many more voices clamoring to be heard in even a small school like Battle Rock, the results were sometimes mixed for teacher and parents alike. As the spring deepened, Kim considered her alternatives, including pulling her daughters out of Battle Rock and educating them at home. Stephen also considered his options but kept them closely guarded secrets from everyone but Susan.

Chapter 17

Innocence Lost

*W*hatever the season, there was a sound heard constantly across Montezuma County. It was heard above the sound of strong winds that sometimes swept through the valley, over the lowing of cattle and braying of horses, and above the sound of the tractors kneading the land. The noise was gunfire.

The distant popping startled me when I first heard it one afternoon while working at home. When I heard the sound again a few seconds later, I remembered John and Brenda Burns and their children hitting the floor of their Cortez home when firecrackers went off at a nearby park, thinking the rat-a-tat was gunfire. But the sounds I heard were most definitely not fireworks. I found my landlord, who lived next door, and asked him if he had heard the gunfire.

"Yeah, probably someone target practicing," he said nonchalantly, as he worked in his yard. "Or maybe they're shooting some wildlife."

In the weeks ahead I heard more gunfire, but like my landlord, few local people gave the noise a second thought. Most of the time, the gunfire was related to hunting, or killing a predator or destroying infirm livestock, or even target practice—all possibilities my landlord offered. I became more aware of the now unmistakable sound, and it occurred to me that spring, when all of Montezuma County, it seemed, was shooting at something, that guns were part of rural life and considered a tool as important as any farm or ranch implement. Which meant that many Montezuma County residents owned firearms with no apologies. Some county residents joined gun leagues, set up like bowling leagues, and others enrolled in gun safety courses. Even children were introduced to guns. When I visited Tim and Staton Jeter one day after school, I watched them practice shooting a tin can off a wood rail fence with a small air rifle. Their father, Chris, stood nearby and taught them about the gun's safety lock, how to aim, and other tips to ensure the boys didn't put out someone's eye or worse.

Of course, in a culture so imbued with guns, neighbors were bound to fire on one another occasionally and sometimes even kill each other. But this was a small town, and murder by firearms was a rarity, which explained why Cortezians were quite unprepared for what transpired at the start of the long and violent Memorial Day weekend in 1998.

*P*aul *Murphy had just parked* the Battle Rock bus at the school district's garage that morning when he heard the piercing sirens and then saw a parade of police cars speeding out of Cortez. He thought an accident had occurred. "I remember walking out to the street and watching all the commotion and wondering what the hell was going on," Paul said. He didn't have to wait long to find out. After leaving the bus garage for a day of errands, he stopped in a store and heard the news over a radio.

"The story was over the scanner that an officer was down and a vehicle was being chased down McElmo Canyon and that the gunmen might be holed up near our home," he said. "I called Battle Rock and fortunately got to talk to Stephen, who told me all the action had already gone by the school and was happening further down the canyon." Paul was relieved the children were safe, but he worried that the gunmen might still be loose in the canyon.

Details of the shooting circulated quickly through the town by word of mouth, and as the sketchy details were firmed, the town confronted the moment when it would never be the same. Dale Claxton was the unfortunate Cortez police officer who spotted a water truck reported stolen earlier in the week. He pulled the truck over as it was leaving town. When he got out of his squad car, a barrage of bullets cut him down.

The gunmen used outlying roads to bypass the town, but they didn't get far before encountering a squad of armed city, county, and state law enforcement officials. The gunmen were only momentarily stopped because they had an advantage: armed with assault weapons, they literally blasted their way past the authorities' guns and rifles. The gunmen escaped into McElmo Canyon, where Stephen was closing out the last day of school.

He and the children witnessed the water truck speed by the school, followed by the screaming sirens of squad cars. People often took the canyon road at high speeds, but the water truck and police and sheriff's cars were traveling fast even by local standards. Everyone froze on the Sticker Patch to watch the curious procession. Most of the children had witnessed a scene like this only on television. Moments later, the school's telephone rang.

When Stephen heard the news, he ordered the children into the school and locked the doors. No one could leave Battle Rock until authorities felt it was safe. Some canyon residents didn't take that chance. They stayed in town that night, unnerved by the prospect that the outlaws might still be hiding in one of McElmo Canyon's numerous nooks and crannies.

That evening and in the days and nights that followed, helicopters flew the canyon's length. Some home owners made sure their guns were loaded and ready for use, if necessary. The Four Corners region was pockmarked with so many canyons that anyone who wanted to hide could easily do so and then prey on people living in remote places; that was the local fear. Despite McElmo Canyon's growth, there were still many isolated homes, and people who didn't own guns, mostly urban people new to the canyon, now purchased firearms and hid them in their homes.

"This happens in a city, not out here in a rural community," said one canyon resident kept awake by the choppers. The sounds of sirens and helicopters were so rare in Montezuma County that when people heard them, they figured the commotion was related to a fire.

And so, while residents fortified themselves, Officer Claxton was laid to rest. The officer's funeral shuttered the town, as several hundred people crowded the football stadium next to the middle school for the service. Paul Murphy also attended and saw tears streaming down the faces of friends and neighbors in the stadium and later, when the funeral cortege slowly made its way down a crowded but eerily silent Main Street. Returning to normalcy was difficult in the weeks that followed, and locals were reminded constantly of the officer's death. Network newscasts and national dailies covered the Claxton murder for weeks for one simple reason: murders of this sort were distressingly common in cities. But in small towns, where people still slept with their doors unlocked, where people knew each other by name, where neighbor helped neighbor, the murder had a man-bites-dog quality. Which is to say the Claxton murder gave the media a new twist on an old story.

The steady stream of news gave Cortez something else to ponder. The murder wasn't committed by outside desperados violating the soul of rural America, as some residents initially believed. Dale Claxton was downed by men from small towns in the region, people like the residents themselves.

Cortezians slept more securely when two of the gunmen were later found dead, one shortly after the furious chase through the canyon, from an apparently self-inflicted gunshot, the remains of the other found more than a year later hidden by brush. The third man remained at large when, fifteen months after Officer Claxton's murder, I moved to Cortez.

I found the town's psyche still shaken. Many residents could tell me where they were and what they were doing the moment they heard the news. Locally, the event carried the same weight as the September 11, 2001, terrorist attack. For others, like Paul and Tumiko Murphy, the incident signaled a sea change to life in a community that had been largely untouched by violence of this magnitude. "It's like the event stripped our feeling of peace and safety," Paul said. With feelings of security gone, some residents began locking their homes at night for the first time in their lives.

*C*uriously, I found the shooting death of Officer Clayton did little to alter rural attitudes about guns. No one I talked to favored gun control, and surveys supported my informal poll. Whereas 60 percent of urban Americans favored tighter control of guns, only 40 percent of rural Americans did, according to a 1997 study conducted for the Hearst newspaper chain. The survey also showed that rural Americans were far more likely to have owned a gun than urban dwellers and 60 percent of rural respondents believed keeping a gun in the home made it safer; only 40 percent of urban residents agreed. Everyone, it seemed, owned a gun, usually a rifle, in Montezuma County, but I was hard-pressed to find anyone who owned as many firearms as Roger Hazlewood.

I first met Roger one Sunday evening after dining with Ed and Alice Baltes, a couple who lived across the road from Roger in one of the canyon's historic stone homes. Roger lived in a modest farmhouse he was restoring, and when Ed and I walked across

the road to say hello, we found him working in his front yard. After our introductions, Roger wasted little time in sharing the latest details of a land dispute with the owner of the neighboring
pasture. As I listened to his story, the feud sounded like a
modern-day version of the Hatfields and McCoys.

Wesley Wallace, a local rancher, had come to talk to him about
a half acre of land that Roger and Wesley both claimed was
theirs. The half acre had once been part of Wesley's pasture. But
the rancher had years ago moved the fence to build a small cor-
ral for his cattle. And when the fence line was moved, Roger acquired the acreage. Roger now considered the property his,
courtesy of Colorado's antiquated fence law. The nineteenth-
century statute essentially said that if a fence stood in the same
place for eighteen years or longer, then that's where the property
line was drawn. No matter what the survey or deed said.

Roger told us he could prove the fence line had been there for
longer than eighteen years. But Wesley was having none of it.
When the rancher had come calling on Roger, the two men began
arguing. Then Wesley took out a pair of leather gloves and
slapped Roger across the face. Roger staggered backwards. Now
pinning Roger against a stone wall, Wesley slapped him again,
this time so hard that Roger said he nearly lost his balance. With
a reddening welt on his face, Roger pulled out a gun hidden in
his pants, pointed it to the ground, and fired once, then a second
time, all the while holding off his bigger and stronger adversary
by putting his hand on Wesley's chest.

I looked at Ed to see his reaction to this story. He gave nothing
away.

"I told him if he didn't get off my land, then the third shot
would end up in him," Roger told us. Wesley's wife, who had accompanied her husband and waited in their pickup truck,
quickly appeared when she heard the gunshots. "After the second shot, Mrs. Wallace came running around the back of the
house. 'You're crazy! You're crazy!' she yelled at me. 'I'm crazy?
You all come on my land, and your husband slaps me, and I'm

crazy?'" She told me she was calling the police. 'Fine,' I said."
Mrs. Wallace didn't care for Roger anyway. "I once referred to
her as Wesley's mother, quite by accident, and she was always
very cool to me after that," said Roger. There was no hint of irony
in his last comment.

"If he comes back, I'm ready for him," Roger told us. With
that, he turned around and lifted his T-shirt to expose a handgun
tucked inside the back of his blue jeans.

"One day, Roger is going to get himself killed," Ed sighed as we
walked back to his house.

A card-carrying member of the National Rifle Association,
Roger owned some thirty guns and rifles. Some were antique,
some were now banned, but the cases in which they were stored
covered a good part of his kitchen floor when I returned alone to
visit for the first time in his home. I walked into his kitchen, sat
down, and noticed a fairly large rifle leaning against the frame of
the kitchen door.

"That's in case he tries to come back," he said, getting up from
a kitchen chair to finger the heavy rifle. In that moment I was
glad not to be Wesley Wallace. "It even has an attachment for a
bayonet, but I don't think I'll be needing that. I told him if he
moved that fence, we would have grief to pay."

When Roger first moved to McElmo Canyon in 1976, he told
everyone he had murdered a man in Arizona. "That scared off a
lot of people, and they left me alone," said Roger.

The story, untrue, did indeed scare people away from Roger
Hazlewood—everyone but Wesley, who continually tried to reclaim his land. On a cold January day in 1999, Wesley showed up
with two of his sons to build a new fence that would reclaim his
half acre.The Denver Broncos were favored that day to retain
their world championship title against the Atlanta Falcons. Anyone in Colorado with a modicum of interest in professional football was glued to his or her television set. Not Wesley Wallace,
intent on taking back what was his.

"I went out with my rifle and just cradled it in my arms while I watched them," Roger said.

Neither side budged that day. Roger kept going in and out of his house, peering at the men sitting in a pickup truck on a frigid day. "They missed two meals. They missed the Super Bowl, and they froze their asses off," said Roger with a smile.

The Wallaces ultimately succeeded in putting up the fence. Roger removed it, cutting through the wire and pulling up the posts. Wesley finally had enough. He filed, and won, a lawsuit against Roger.

When Roger saw Wesley at a local supermarket, he congratulated the rancher on his hard-fought win. The months-long land squabble and the shooting helped cement Roger's reputation as someone who embodied rural sensibilities about guns, even though the canyon's newer residents from cities were put off by his behavior. Not that he cared what his neighbors thought. He figured he was only standing up for what was rightfully his. In McElmo Canyon that sometimes meant taking up a gun or rifle to shoo off an ornery neighbor, as he had on another occasion a few years earlier. The neighbor, intent on clearing the irrigation ditch of the towering willows that grew in and along the banks, planned to use Agent Orange.

"We went to war over Agent Orange," said Roger, a Vietnam veteran, who recognized the chemicals for Agent Orange stored on a trailer behind his neighbor's tractor. "They didn't even know what they had. I told him he wasn't spraying my land with that. He went away and then came back a few days later, and said, 'Roger, I'm going to spray those willows,' and I had my gun in my arms, and we came to a meeting of the minds. He didn't spray, and I didn't shoot."

Roger, however, smelled Agent Orange in the wind a few days later from his neighbor spraying upstream. Two days later, Roger's vegetable garden was flattened.

*D*espite the occasional warning shots at neighbors, attention to gun safety in rural America ran high. People generally knew how to use and care for them. But for all the precautions, devastating accidents still occurred.

Three months after Officer Claxton was gunned down, another death jolted canyon residents. Sheldon and Naomi Zwicker lived at the far end of the canyon, pursuing relatively secluded lives that revolved around their cattle business. But a spring cleaning of an irrigation ditch of willows and weeds unearthed a handgun. One of the couple's sons took it home and began cleaning it one night at the dining-room table, unaware that the chamber was loaded. The gun discharged and struck another Zwicker son in the head. Eleven-year-old Kona was doing math homework.

Fatally wounded, the boy was airlifted to a Grand Junction hospital. During the flight, with his mother at his side, he slipped into a coma. Sheldon meanwhile made the four-hour drive to Grand Junction to be with his son and wife, unaware that his son was dying. By the time Sheldon arrived, the boy was gone.

What happened next was straight from the pages of an America long gone in most places, for the land that helped sustain the boy in life served as his resting place in death. Sheldon had the hospital put his son in a body bag and place him in the back seat of the car. Accompanied by a friend, Sheldon drove himself and his son back to McElmo Canyon. He called home before he left Grand Junction, and in a conference call the family decided they would bury Kona on their land, without the assistance of a funeral home or embalmers.

By the time Sheldon arrived in the canyon early the next morning, preparations were complete. Neighbors had excavated a grave and built a simple casket. The boy was wrapped in several Navajo blankets that friends had given the family for the occasion. Audrey Allmon played hymns on a portable keyboard moved near the grave. With the tender good-byes of his family, he was lowered into the ground. The family gathered at the casket and cried.

"We touched him and said good-bye," said Sheldon. "I threw the first handful of dirt."

He was buried alongside a grandmother and an infant brother. Elsewhere on the Zwicker homestead, yet another infant son was buried under the broad boughs of a tree. Burying your own dead was still possible under Colorado law, if you buried the deceased within twenty-four hours of passing and if authorities determined there was no foul play.

More than a year after Kona's death, Sheldon talked about the accidental shooting death of his son with a reserved comportment that suggested time had made his wounds more manageable. A color photograph of the boy looked out over the dining-room table.

"That was the hardest thing that could happen to a parent," Sheldon said. "But I don't blame guns for what happened to my son."

In rural communities, there was a vehement opposition to gun control, even in the wake of the 1999 Columbine High School shootings. Thirteen people were killed at the suburban Denver school, including the two gunmen, who were students. Urban opinion ran high in favor of tighter laws, but not in rural America, not in McElmo Canyon. Arguing for stricter control of guns made as much sense as putting out a welcome mat for all the urban people moving to Montezuma County. The notion was unthinkable.

Chapter 18

"It's Good to Make Your Own Way"

I sat behind the steering wheel of the idling pickup truck and looked straight ahead at a herd of cattle on the road. There was no opening in the herd, there was no breeze, and the air reeked. That's when I heard Audrey Allmon yelling directions.

"They aren't going to move for you! You have to bump them!" she hollered. Audrey, Battle Rock's former teacher, was holding open a gate for me, behind which stood dozens of cattle in no rush to clear the gravel road.

"Bump them!" she ordered. "You won't hurt them!"

I cautiously stepped on the gas and drove slowly through the stubborn cattle, their moos rising in protest as I literally pushed through them and over the fresh mounds of manure. The tires made a squishing sound as I drove over the patties and past the gate. Romantic notions about cattle drives, I decided, were best set aside.

Audrey joined me in the truck, and we drove through the length of the herd until we found Sheldon and Naomi Zwicker preparing for the first day of their cattle drive, a project that would take us and five hundred cattle over thirty-five miles to fresh mountain pastures. The Zwickers had spent the night in a small trailer, with the best view I had seen yet of the Sleeping Ute Mountain, draped in a verdant cloak. After the Zwickers secured the contents of the trailer, which also served as the chuck wagon, the cattle began moving toward the gate through which I had just passed. Beyond the gate was the gravel road that would take the herd through the heart of Montezuma County en route to their pastures. I found myself sitting in the passenger seat of one of the Zwickers' pickup trucks as Naomi drove us toward the restless herd and the gate that, when it was finally opened again, signaled the start of the drive. Naomi inched down the gravel road teeming with flies lighting on the cow pies. The moos from the cattle were deafening.

"Sometimes they get separated, and the calves and the cows know each others' moos and smells," she told me as she drove through the herd toward the gate. "Right now, they're mellow. The moos also mean they are discontent. They're just standing here, and ready to go."

It all sounded like noise to me, but as someone who had spent no time around cattle, I took Naomi at her word that the bawling and moos actually meant something. The cows became quiet, then one corner of the herd began bawling again, and the bellowing rolled through different sections of the herd like a sort of complicated musical score. As she slowly drove through the sea of cattle, Naomi banged the side of the driver's door to roust the cows from the road. They parted for her more quickly than they had for me. Several yards ahead, Sheldon sat on his mount. He opened the gate, and the drive was on.

We were overtaken by the rushing cattle, impatient to get to their pastures on land the Zwickers leased from the government in the cool Colorado mountains. The cattle traveled along the sides of the road, through the sagebrush, as they raised a cloud of dust that would always seem to hang over the herd as we made our way from pasture to pasture. Sheldon and several other family members and friends watched the edges of the herd, and it was soon apparent why. New calves quickly fell behind, their tiny legs unaccustomed to being driven over the rough terrain.

"Eeeeee! Git!" yelled Elsie, one of the Zwickers' daughters, as several calves tried to turn into the brush. The sound of her voice and the towering horse turned the calves back into the herd. Once the drive was underway, Naomi joined it on horseback, leaving me to drive the family's pickup. I soon realized why it took five days to travel just thirty-five miles. The heat took its toll on the cattle, and the journey was even harder on the calves. After three short hours, the Zwickers stopped to rest.

The drive held an appeal to tourists, who stopped to take photographs or videotape the procession, but locals observed the herd for other reasons. When the drive resumed after about an hour, home owners came out on porches, and several of them stood at their property line to discourage the cattle from trampling their lawns. One woman stood behind a broken-down section of her wood rail fence that protected a flawless green lawn fronting her double-wide home. I stopped the pickup truck for a visit.

"I'm standing here so that no more cows come into my yard," the woman told me. She wore a T-shirt that featured profiles of turkeys, and didn't appear in the least to mind the disruption created by noisy cattle now parading by her property. "This is still the way to go, as far as I'm concerned. I've nearly been run over by too many cattle trucks."

She was right. In driving across the West, I had also nearly been run over by speeding eighteen-wheelers trucking cattle to market or to fresh pasture. Trucking cattle was faster, and the animals lost less weight than driving them the traditional way. But there was another good reason for driving cattle the old-fashioned way, and it had to do with money. Earlier, Sheldon had told me that the family saved several hundred dollars; trucking them would have added $1,500 on top of the cash the Zwickers were already out for all the gas for their pickup trucks and the food and ice to operate the chuck wagon. This year, the Zwickers paid dearly for their thrift when the late spring turned unseasonably warm. All of us, including the cows, suffered when the temperature soared to one hundred degrees on the first day and nearly hit the century mark the second day.

Saving money, however, had become more difficult because of the rapidly disappearing range. In the Zwickers' case, pastures available just a year ago were now fenced off, sold to developers, or urban people, or farmers who planned to sow crops on the dormant fields. When Audrey returned to the pickup I was driving, she talked about the development of once vacant land. "I don't know how many more years we'll be able to do this. We used to pasture there last year," she said, pointing to one fenced-off field the family had long used. "This might be the last year."

The disappearance of open range stemmed from Montezuma County's growth, which generated another problem for the Zwickers. Motorists, more and more of them new to rural America, were less inclined to sit on the highway to let the lumbering cattle cross. I had read a story months earlier in the *Cortez Journal* about how one motorist approaching a bluff apparently didn't see, or ignored, a cattleman waving a flag to warn drivers a herd was on the other side of the hill. The motorist slammed into the man and his horse. The man was thrown from his mount and suffered a broken collarbone and shoulder blade and fractured ribs. His seriously injured horse was destroyed, and the motorist was ticketed for careless driving. There was a perilous side to driving cattle, and errant motorists were just the beginning.

During the drive's first morning, Naomi's horse threw her to the ground. She was sore, but her injuries would have been worse had her shoulder not absorbed most of the impact.

"Well, you don't look the worse for wear," Sheldon told his wife as we ate a hamburger lunch that day in the sweltering chuck wagon. "I guess it's that hard head of yours," he said, smiling at her. Humor often helped the Zwickers through the demanding drive.

The heat lifted on Tuesday evening, as the herd lumbered across State Highway 145. The sight was a curious one: cattle walked around and between pickup trucks, long flatbeds loaded with harvested logs for home construction, late-model cars, and sport utility vehicles—all stalled by the cows. The herd had become divided during the drive, the heat slowing down the calves and less resilient cattle. The slower cattle stopped to rest, while the other half of the herd made good time to a small pasture across Highway 145. About forty-five minutes later, the rest of the herd appeared on the horizon, their bawling carried on the cooling wind to the pasture.

Cows already in the fenced area began mooing, as many of them went to the fence, looking at the other half of the approaching herd. The pasture became bedlam as cows and calves were noisily reunited. Within an hour, the pasture was relatively quiet, as calves settled into nursing and their mothers contentedly chewed on grass at the end of the hard, hot, long day. The drive was a drill in patience and stamina, and anyone who went along for the first time came away with new appreciation for red meat.

*M*ore than any family in McElmo Canyon, the Zwickers *were* rural America. The family had called the canyon home for three generations, a time span that had allowed the family's eighty-six-year-old patriarch, Eldon Zwicker, to amass the six thousand acres managed by his three sons. Among those sons, no one cast a larger shadow than fifty-seven-year-old Sheldon Zwicker. Several weeks after visiting the elder Mr. Zwicker and weeks before the cattle drive, I paid a visit to Sheldon and his family.

Sheldon and Naomi lived three miles past Battle Rock school, past several farms and not far from the Utah state line. I drove up a long, narrow gravel road to the family's farmhouse. Roosters and chickens wandered the yard, and in the distance, palominos grazed with some of the family's cattle in a tree-studded pasture. The simple frame house was nearly a century old and had been built by Sheldon's grandfather. The dwelling still had the original tin roof. The family's homestead was strictly utilitarian.

"We would like to live this style of life for as long as we can," Naomi told me after she greeted me at the screen door that opened to her kitchen. "All of us know we can sell off our land and live high off the hog."

Sheldon soon joined us at the family's dining-room table. He was dressed in a white T-shirt, crisp blue jeans, and boots. He added that they planned to keep their land intact so that their children and grandchildren could build houses when they came of age. "We don't want people living next to us that we don't know," Sheldon said firmly.

That was one way to shield themselves from McElmo Canyon's growth, which had transformed the place more in the last decade than in the previous four. One day a few years earlier, as Sheldon drove home after a trip to town, he told me he pretended he was driving through the canyon for the first time in twenty years. Two decades earlier, the road was gravel. Most of the land, unsettled. "I tricked myself so well, I was shaking. Every place that there had been one or two houses, there were now seven or eight homes. I used to know everyone in the canyon. We don't really see the change every year—there's only one or two new homes," he said. "I knew everyone in the canyon and was related to everyone. In Battle Rock, I was related to most of the kids one year."

He spoke the truth. When Sheldon was a seventh grader in
1957, he was related to twenty-three of his twenty-seven classmates. There was a time when Battle Rock itself was the embodiment of the Zwickers. Sheldon's grandmother was in the
school's first class, and the school's second teacher, Mary Taylor,
boarded with Sheldon's grandparents in the very house in which
Sheldon and Naomi now lived. Now Sheldon only knew two, perhaps three, children at the school. And it was around school issues—beginning with the uproar over the construction of
modern bathrooms—that the Zwickers got the first inkling of
change that soon swept through the school and, later, the canyon
itself.

"I preferred the old way—history, geography, math, old hard-
line curriculum. It prepared you for business and the world,"
said Sheldon. Although he acknowledged schools today provided
"a more balanced education," he still thought the offerings vio-
lated his personal tastes. After all the collisions between rural
and urban parents, followed by the Botticelli mess and the hom-
age paid to insects through the Battle Rock Bug Club, the Zwickers decided to home school their children.

The couple had purchased an old bookmobile, complete with
several hundred books, to educate their children. The bookmobile was driven out to the fields during harvests, and during
breaks, Naomi convened classes amid the bales of hay. These
days the bookmobile sat unused in a corner of the Zwickers'
land, not far from the house. As we visited, the couple's youngest
daughter sat at the table doing homework.

No longer members of the Battle Rock school community, the
Zwickers had withdrawn to their farm and ranch operation,
where, as far as I could tell, they never compromised a lifestyle
as basic as the house in which they lived.

Sheldon was up most mornings before the sun spilled over the
canyon's ragged outcroppings, and he worked until dark, plant-
ing and plowing fields, moving cattle from one pasture to another, and making sure water flowed unobstructed through the

irrigation ditch. The work was strenuous and dangerous, judging from the injuries that Sheldon endured.

Sheldon and Naomi were harvesting hay in 1992 on Father's Day when Sheldon suddenly felt one of the baler's steel rods puncture the top of his boot and run straight through his foot. Naomi was on the other side of the noisy machine and couldn't see or hear her husband writhing in pain. When she finally realized what had happened, she rushed Sheldon to the house. They soaked his foot in kerosene, which prevented infection.

A steel rod through a foot was bad enough, but on another occasion, Sheldon lost the tips of two fingers when machinery sliced them off. He retrieved his fingertips and, with Naomi driving, went to Southwest Memorial Hospital in Cortez. Sheldon had hoped to get them reattached, but the hospital denied him care because he didn't have health insurance.

"There's nothing like getting your fingers cut off," said Sheldon, holding out his right hand for me to see. Two of the fingers were noticeably shorter. But the misfortune was part and parcel of a life that made steel rods in a foot and sliced fingertips mere inconveniences.

"It's a clean lifestyle, and you're your own boss," he said. "The freedom is invaluable. It's good to make your own way. We have a garden, and our own animals."

Naomi nodded in agreement. "There's a sense of fulfillment when you live this way," she said. "You sustain yourself. I feel totally free. You become part of the land, and the land becomes part of you."

The family so valued self-sufficiency that they took their setbacks in stride, including the fights with neighbors that became local lore. Sheldon stood five feet, eight inches tall and weighed all of 155 pounds. But he was powerfully built, his biceps straining the sleeves of his T-shirt. He kept in shape by punching the tires of his tractor, which produced those Popeye-like biceps any muscle magazine would have been proud to put on its cover. Pummeling tractor tires also produced a broad chest, a washboard stomach, and a thirty-two-inch waist—all of which spelled trouble for a neighbor one day.

The neighbor, a local businessman, had beaten up Sheldon's big brother in a dispute over property lines and grazing. The man trounced Sherman so badly that he lay in a pasture unconscious for several hours before other family members found him. Sheldon vowed to find his neighbor and teach him a lesson. He wasn't one for idle threats.

As Sheldon and Naomi drove a narrow gravel back road in Montezuma County, they happened on their neighbor driving the same road. There wasn't enough room for both vehicles to pass at the same time, so both men stopped. Sheldon made his move.

He walked over to the neighbor's pickup and said, "I need to talk to you."

Sitting in the pickup a few feet away, Naomi remembered watching Sheldon's fist going through his neighbor's open window. Naomi rushed to her husband and their now bleeding neighbor. More words were exchanged, and Sheldon went at his bleeding neighbor again with another flurry of fists.

"I hung on to Sheldon and said, 'That's enough,'" said Naomi. "I was scared. I had never seen anyone bleed so much. There was blood everywhere!"

There was no more trouble about property boundaries, grazing, or anything else, for that matter. When I called the Zwickers' neighbor, he declined to talk about the incident and hung up. Four years after the back-road skirmish, Sheldon talked about the pummeling with a disarming directness that I had come to appreciate as a hallmark of longtime rural residents. "If someone needs a spanking, then they need a spanking," he told me. "If you don't treat me with respect, then I am going to whip you. I'm going to take you to the dirt."

By his own account, Sheldon figured he had taken "several" people to the dirt as a younger man, but only "four" in the last twenty years. He credited his wife with calming him down. Besides, there was livestock to tend, fields to cultivate, and in the spring, cattle drives to summer pastures.

*A*s *I prepared for the cattle drive,* my plan was to stay with the family day and night. I borrowed a sleeping bag and bought bug spray, sun block, and a $5 straw hat at Wal-Mart. I quickly changed my mind about sleeping outdoors when Audrey told me she planned to drive home each night.

"I've slept on the hard ground, in rain and in snow," she told me. "I don't need to do it anymore."

I decided I didn't need to do it at all. I hitched a ride back to her house and then drove myself home. When I got home at the end of a very long first day, I collapsed in my bed fully clothed. I had no problem whatsoever in acknowledging that I needed indoor plumbing, a comfortable bed, and a hot morning shower.

By midweek the heat broke. But the cooler weather was the only break the Zwickers had on a day that started bad. A heifer fractured one of her front legs, and Sheldon moved the big white cow with black spots to a friend's nearby pasture and left her there. He later returned to find the thirsty cow had hobbled into a nearby pond for a drink. In the process of trying to free herself from the muddy bottom, she had broken the leg. The heifer was removed with a backhoe, but now she was unable to even hobble. Sheldon made a decision he didn't like. He shot the cow behind its right ear and then dragged her to an isolated place on the farm. The buzzards and coyotes ate well that week.

"The older I get, the more difficult it is for me to do that," he told me after he killed the cow. "That heifer really was trying, and she wanted to rejoin the herd, but she just couldn't do it."

As the cattle continued their forced march, they became so tightly bunched in the road that motorists had a difficult time driving through the herd. There was always the danger of cattle scratching paint jobs, or worse. Naomi came into the chuck wagon with this news as Audrey and I worked on lunch. I had signed on as Audrey's assistant cook, and we had spent the better part of the morning preparing Navajo tacos.

"They could have kicked out a headlight," said Audrey, who sliced tomatoes as I diced lettuce at the trailer's tiny table. "It could have been a disaster."

"It was a wreck," Naomi concurred.

"But you can't appreciate the good days without a few bad ones," said Audrey, smiling. The former teacher recycled her treasury of platitudes from Battle Rock for the cattle drive.

Naomi agreed.

Later that day, cattle wandered onto lawns and into pastures. Exasperated by the wandering cattle, some residents called the Montezuma County Sheriff's Department to complain. Audrey knew the sheriff personally and called him to smooth things over. But after cattle trampled one man's lawn, he leveled harsh words at Naomi.

"Sir, you don't have to talk to me that way," she told the man. "I have apologized."

Then Sheldon went to the man to apologize.

"Keep them out of my flowers," the man said. "I know you all just want free pasture."

"We have all the pasture we need," Sheldon retorted, apologizing again.

The man kept complaining. Sheldon's blue eyes turned menacing. He set his jaw and became firm with the man. The home owner, knowing full well Sheldon Zwicker's reputation for punching out people, saw the look. He turned away. The conversation was over.

"Have a good afternoon," the man told Sheldon.

"I was about to tell him I had apologized twice and did he want an ass whooping," said Sheldon, who later recounted the story over lunch in the chuck wagon.

Two other families called the sheriff's department about the herd, as if the Zwickers needed more headaches. Gone were the days, it seemed, when neighbors and property owners were tolerant. Many of the newcomers who had taken up residence in big, sparkling country homes had no patience for cows rumbling across their manicured lawns and flower beds, knocking down fences and gates, and leaving behind enough manure, it seemed, to fertilize the field at Yankee Stadium for a decade.

The Zwickers made a practice of reimbursing property owners for any damage their cattle inflicted. But that still didn't stop angry residents some years from shooting at the herd or the Zwickers. That didn't happen on this drive, but hostile gunfire explained why they carried guns. Two rifles, in fact, were stored beneath the seat in one of the Zwickers' pickups. When Audrey opened the door of the vehicle one day to retrieve bottled water, she noticed the rifles poking out from under the seat.

"Oh, shoot," she said, laughing a bit nervously. "I hope I don't blow off my foot." She was actually lucky she hadn't lost a few fingers or one of her hands. Her keys were bundled on a key chain that sported a live bullet.

On Friday the family had the help of more cow punchers—friends and volunteers—and it was a good thing. Before the herd lay the town of Dolores, which we passed through en route to our mountain pasture destination. I was recruited for flagging duty. The job of a flagger seemed simple enough, but it was a fairly important one. Parked on the highway's shoulder just behind where the cattle were entering the road, I waved a yellow caution flag outside the driver's window to warn approaching motorists of cattle they would soon encounter. When the cows were safely on the highway, I followed them slowly into Dolores.

Shopkeepers came out and stood on the wood plank sidewalks. They waved at the Zwickers and the cowpokes helping the family. Thoroughly into the moment, I waved back. The herd moved slowly down Railroad Avenue, the town's main street, and past the Naked Moose Café, Wagon West ("Happy Gifts From the West"), and the appropriately named Trailside General Store. Tourists from Florida, Georgia, Pennsylvania, Texas, and California gawked at the drive. Some of them stopped their vehicles to get photographs of themselves with the cattle in the background. I posed for one photograph, decked in my Wal-Mart straw hat.

As the cattle made their way through town, I listened to a Cortez country-and-western radio station whose slogan reminded listeners that "mending fences, branding cattle goes better with KRTZ-FM 98.7 on your dial." The station repeatedly played one tune about a rural family confounded by the urbanization of the American countryside. "Daddy Won't Sell the Farm" lamented the construction of malls, parking lots, and fast-food restaurants encroaching on a family farm. The song could have been written for and about the Zwickers.

By sundown we had reached our destination. Seated on his horse and stripped to his waist, Sheldon was browned by the sun and hoarse from yelling at cattle. As the sun began its descent, Sheldon knew it was setting on more than just the day. Earlier in the drive, I had asked him how many more years the family could drive its cattle in country more populated and less tolerant of rural traditions.

"Not many more," Sheldon responded.

He knew the American West he loved was vanishing.

Chapter 19

The Vanishing West

*O*ver the rim of McElmo Canyon, no more than a dozen miles, as the crows fly, from where the Zwickers lived, lay a hint of what, perhaps, awaited much of Montezuma County: a twelve-hundred-acre development that billed itself on a large sales sign as "Americas First Archeological Subdivision." *Americas* didn't have an apostrophe, but who cared about punctuation when you were selling prehistoric history along with thirty-five-acre home sites, which is exactly what developer Archie Hanson was doing with Indian Camp Ranch.

Montezuma County's first gated community had eighty recorded Anasazi ruins, from kivas to homes, towers, granaries, and middens, the garbage heaps where the ancient people dumped their broken pottery, bones from the animals they ate, and as it happened, their dead. At $3,000 an acre, Archie Hanson, who was no relation to teacher Stephen Hanson, guaranteed at least one ruin on each home site in the development that boasted vistas of the Sleeping Ute Mountain, Mesa Verde, and in the distance, the La Plata Mountains, which were snowcapped nearly year-round. By the spring of 2000, all but ten of the thirty-two home sites were sold, without a penny of advertising, and Archie was on the verge of boosting prices again, jumping a $145,000 home site by $30,000. If average sales prices of undeveloped land in Montezuma County were increasing, and they were, Archie and other people like him, for better or worse, had a big hand in it.

When I arrived for a tour, Archie was waiting outside the sprawling two-story home he shared with his wife, Mary. He was wearing a broad-brimmed straw hat and a canvas-colored shirt boasting the name of his development. We boarded a luxurious maroon-colored Ford Expedition, which also bore the name of Indian Camp Ranch. The Expedition vaguely resembled the vehicles used in the movie *Jurassic Park*.

Archie drove the gravel roads of his development, stopping at intersections to explain his vision. "We had no role model for what we're doing here, so we really had to think about it," he said. "People are looking at us very closely. We're not fooling. This has got to set a standard, otherwise we become the very thing people have criticized us for initially."

If he was defensive on first meeting, he had good reason. The local paper, mirroring the sentiments of the local populace, had lambasted his development and the evil it represented: more growth, more traffic, higher land prices. "When I first got here, I was reviled. Everyone said, 'Here comes another developer, and he's going to ruin everything.' I was criticized a lot, but I didn't really care. But it got to where Mary couldn't read the paper."

In selling his Indian Camp Ranch as the country's "first archeological development," Archie struck a marketing mother lode that caught locals by utter surprise. Cortezians, though proud of the region's ancient history, were also mostly nonchalant about using the regional color. At first, locals laughed at the Californian when he announced plans to develop the land as a high-end development built around the Anasazi mystique. Locals weren't laughing now, but they were keeping a keen eye on the developer. Archie stopped the expedition, and we walked to one of the last unsold home sites.

"Look at the paint on this pottery," he said, handing me a shard with an intricate design in black highlighted by a band of red paint still clearly evident around the rim of what had probably been a cup. "Imagine a paint company today being able to boast its product lasts a thousand years."

Archie got back to his point, namely the local opposition to his development. "They all said, 'Who's going to buy there?'" Locals didn't have to wait long to find out.

People with a lot of money flocked to Indian Camp Ranch. Those who bought into Archie's dream were big names with deep pockets, like Bob Greenlee, the former mayor of Boulder, Colorado, who gave $9 million to the Iowa State University journalism school. "He has serious money," said Archie as we continued our tour of his development and he recited name after name of well-heeled people who had purchased his thirty-five-acre home sites. One wealthy woman couldn't decide which parcel she wanted, Archie told me, so she bought two.

Only a handful of houses had been erected, and at every point we stopped, the views were somewhere beyond picturesque. At one point, Archie created a road where there wasn't one, and we bounced in the cab of the Expedition as he drove through what once had been farm- and pastureland. He squeezed the four-wheel-drive vehicle through dense growth of cedar and juniper. We stopped near a field and walked, as he continued to talk. I was enthralled by the pottery shards that littered the ground. I picked them up, ignoring local warnings about removing anything from these ancient sites. Odd things happen, rural and urban residents alike warned me, when you took shards or anything else from these ancient settlements. Native Americans didn't go near the ruins. They believed the spirits of the onetime residents still resided in the tumbled walls.

"Take them if you like," Archie told me as I inspected one

shard. You could take anything ancient from private land, he told me, but federal law banned the removal of artifacts from public land.

Archie returned to more-grounded topics, like the intense scrutiny he faced from locals. He was mindful of locals' opinions, and he asked the same of people who bought in Indian Camp Ranch. Although the ruins and pots and cups that some residents found on their land were theirs, Archie prohibited the sale of artifacts as part of the purchase agreement. Violators faced stiff fines from Archie.

"You could take a complete pot and sell it for $30,000 at Sotheby's. It would go for that much because the market's there. But that's not what we're about."

Archie had discovered Montezuma County like a lot of urban people before him: on family vacations. He had come to Montezuma County by way of California, the son of a prominent landscape gardener and author whose work had been featured in the *Los Angeles Times Magazine*. Archie Hanson's father came from money, and Archie Hanson Jr. grew up in Beverly Hills and attended the University of California at Los Angeles, where his fraternity brother was John Ehrlichman, who later served as President Nixon's legal counsel. Hanson later shared a boat with Ehrlichman and Bob Haldeman, later Nixon's chief of staff. He had rubbed elbows with Ronald and Nancy Reagan, Clare Boothe Luce, several movie stars, and other rich and famous Californians.

"We were mixed up with all them at one time," said Archie, as the tour ended and we entered his home. "Ronald Reagan is my hero."

The Hansons had taken up residence two years earlier in Indian Camp Ranch, in a two-story house. The dwelling was partly constructed of stones from Anasazi ruins that the couple bought as salvage from farmers who tore down the ruins to farm their land. The Hansons' home also had unbroken views of the nearby mountains, as well as Shiprock, fifty miles away, thanks to the number of ceiling-to-floor windows. The house had a second floor, and the dwelling was topped by a caramel-brown tin roof, under which sprawled 4,800 square feet—more space than two people needed, Archie admitted,"but whenever we ran into trouble, we just budged the walls out."

Off one long hallway, a large window looked out over a 175-square-foot parcel of land to a sight so extraordinary that I stood there for a moment, utterly stunned by what lay before me. Beneath the open-air shelter lay rock-strewn earth that, as layers of dirt had been removed, yielded an entire Anasazi village—twenty-eight rooms, a kiva, a two-story house, and a tower. "A whole complete village," said Archie, looking out the hallway window at the work in progress. "We're going to run tours through the village when we finish the excavation."

There were other new developments and high-end housing sprouting across Montezuma County, including in McElmo Canyon, but none rivaled Indian Camp Ranch's marketing efforts.

"A lot of the real estate ads in the paper advertise 'Anasazi Ruins,' and that means bring a pick and shovel," he said. At Indian Camp Ranch, Archie hired a small band of archeologists, who had labeled every ruin on the development. The Hansons had five archeological reports alone on the village that was slowly being unearthed next to their house.

There was a secret about Montezuma County, which Archie Hanson as a developer knew, that made Indian Camp Ranch possible. In unregulated Colorado, fully a third of the state's sixty-three counties had no building code. Much of the West was still largely unencumbered that way, and the absence of red tape allowed Archie to develop Indian Camp Ranch in a fraction of the seven years he estimates it would have taken him to secure all the permits to launch a similar venture in California. Archie felt free in Montezuma County, in much the same way other urbanites felt when they arrived in this land of canyons and rolling farmland.

Relaxed property covenants and the absence of building codes at Indian Camp Ranch also meant that landowners could build any sort of dwelling on their land, and many did. The sites yielded sprawling adobe homes, ranch-style houses, and high-end log homes with garages that were larger than many homes in nearby Cortez.

"But death unto you if you put up a trailer home," said Archie, who didn't care what kind of home his buyers erected on their land so long as it wasn't a mobile home. "Trailer homes fly in the face of quality." Which meant a good number of Cortezians, if they could afford to buy the land, couldn't have scraped together enough money to build.

*E*scalating real estate prices were the most discernable impact of Montezuma County's population boom. Though prices varied wildly, depending on whether property had access to water, utilities, and views, McElmo Canyon's real estate began climbing steadily in the 1990s, recording gains as steep as anywhere. The run-up in prices turned a run-down 103-year-old stone house that sat on four acres into a gold mine for Ed and Alice Baltes. They bought the broken-down house for $40,000 in 1994. Five years later, the dwelling and the land could have fetched $225,000.

The Baltes home sat in a small clearing surrounded on three sides by huge boulders. Six gables looked out like friendly eyes, and the stone chimney rose ten feet above the steep pitch of the maroon-colored shingled roof. The front fence was laden with the leafy growth of a fragrant trumpet vine. A wraparound porch, the top of which served as a balcony for three second-floor bedrooms, embraced the front of the house. The simple square construction was softened by a fanciful growth of wisteria that traveled up the porch posts to the balcony and wrapped itself around the railing.

"It's a labor of love," said Ed, strolling through the garden that surrounded the house, which sat just a few miles from Battle Rock school, where he served on the school board and where his grandchildren had attended. "We've done a lot of work on it. But we aren't finished by any means."

The couple considered the house a find unlike any other, even though the county had condemned it. The house leaned and sagged when they bought it and was overrun with rats, mice, chipmunks, squirrels, and other animals. The foundation was compromised. The floors gave underfoot. All of which prompted Montezuma County officials to condemn the property in 1990. Add to that the fact there had been a suicide in the house shortly before the county declared it unsafe, and well, there weren't many folks besides Ed and Alice who were interested in the place. They fell in love with the eyesore and bought it. Some of their friends wondered whether the couple had overpaid for a house that not only was a wreck but had a violent history to boot.

"We saw potential," said Ed. Even he had to admit it took a sharp eye to see that potential.

By the time the couple bought their home, anything on four legs that could fit through the stones and crumbling adobe had tunneled through virtually every inch of the house. This freeway of tunnels, of course, led to nests of every kind. Once, when Alice was working to remove the crumbling century-old adobe mortar so the stone wall could be strengthened with modern concrete, a fat rat jumped out of the wall. She screamed, retreating to the kitchen. Ed took a shovel to the interloper. At night, the scampering in the walls and under the floor often awakened them. They pressed on, until they saw a six-foot bull snake slither out of their dream home. They moved back into their trailer, which sat next to the house, surrendering their home for a time to varmints and snakes. The snake wasn't poisonous, but even so. "It doesn't give you a lot of confidence to see a snake come out of your house," said Ed. "It's a constant battle against the critter element."

Others relocating to rural communities didn't cozy up to the wildlife, and they made as much noise as the animals did. They whined about trash cans overturned by nocturnal animals, roosters crowing in predawn hours, deer and raccoons raiding gardens, trampling young plants while devouring others—all intolerable inconveniences that they hadn't faced in their cities. But the battle between human beings and wildlife came to a head in New York state.

Many people bailed out of cities like New York, Buffalo, and Rochester in the 1990s to find tranquility in the countryside, a land, as it happened, largely made up of working farms and home to a host of varmints. Rural folks laughed at urbanites trying to fit in, but in New York, at least, the persnickety city people had the last word. They grumbled so loud and so often to their lawmakers that in the 1990s New York became the first state in the country to pass a law that required real estate agents to tell potential urban buyers that rural living had pluses and minuses and what they were. The urban expectation that life in rural America had to be free of inconveniences like wild animals created friction between rural and urban families. There were other wars between rural and urban—battles over property lines, for instance—but none rankled rural folks more deeply than that over urbanites trying to remake the land.

Ed was ultimately handier, with a hammer, than the animals were in gaining entry. The couple also didn't mind the wildlife, having grown up in rural America. Ed, raised on an Iowa farm, and Alice, reared in the small Michigan town of Port Huron, had come to these parts by way of Arizona and then Utah. A corporate restructuring pushed Ed and Alice deep into McElmo Canyon and back to lifestyles they had once fully embraced in childhood. They enjoyed reclaiming the old house, which five years later was one of the best examples of restoration work on McElmo Canyon's old stone houses.

The Baltes homestead actually had two dwellings other than the trailer. A smaller house, which was built first, sat to the right of the Baltes home and had served as a rest stop in the 1890s for the wagon trains and the stage coach traveling between Dolores, Colorado, and Bluff, Utah. There were few dwellings in the canyon with as much history and lore as the Baltes home, and few, if any, had as many ghosts.

Alice felt the spirits' presence from time to time, as she did her housework or made bread or canned vegetables or peaches, and sometimes she caught their presence in movement she saw from the corner of her eye. Things moved and things disappeared with no explanation and with such regularity that Ed and Alice eventually simply shrugged off the occurrences, as did their guests.

One night, the couple hosted a dinner party to which I was invited. Also on the guest list was the Balteses' psychic friend from Farmington, New Mexico. Kathleen told us that night that the Baltes home was haunted. I looked around the table at the reactions. People nodded as if they were agreeing with a comment about nice weather.

A century after their murders, Kathleen told us, the spirits of two men still resided in dark corners of the smaller, sod-roofed dwelling. Ed used the smaller structure as storage. He went in and out of the place often. But Alice absolutely refused to step foot in the structure.

"I don't feel comfortable there," she said.

For good reason, Kathleen replied. "They were not nice people."

Ollie, however, was amenable, and his spirit still lived in the big house with Ed and Alice, said Kathleen. The gay man and his partner ran the Magic Flute Trading Post out of the house for several years, selling antiques and other odds and ends to passersby. But when Ollie's partner left him, the man committed suicide by hanging himself from the rickety spiral staircase that Ed and Alice removed, replacing it with a more conventional stairway.

"Ollie's still here," said Ed. "He liked to be called Lance. He's an okay guy."

In addition to Ollie, a Ute Indian chief also claimed the Baltes house as his home. At times the home *felt* crowded. One night when Kathleen house-sat for the couple, she fastened the two locks on the door to Ed's workshop, an enclosed porch off the living room, and went to sleep. She awoke when she got cold and found the door to the workshop standing wide open. On another occasion, Kathleen's dog got up when Alice walked into the living room—originally the home's kitchen—and the animal intently stared at the wall, not at Alice.

"Animals can see entities, too," she said the night she dined with Ed and Alice. "You never see them directly; they always appear as a sudden movement in the corner of your eyes or as a mist. And when you walk through them, the air is chilled."

Spirits or no, Ed declared to Kathleen and the rest of us that there was plenty of room for everyone in the two-story house. He didn't mind the odd item found out of place on more days than he could count.

Buying an old house also included other features that most home buyers didn't have and probably didn't want. Ed and Alice's dream home also included a cemetery plot that was now home for the original owner, James D. Lamb, who had purchased 160 acres of McElmo Canyon land in 1892. In addition to Mr. Lamb, other family members rested behind a solidly constructed chain-link fence. I accompanied Ed on a walking tour of the property, and it ended at the cemetery.

The graves, dug in McElmo Canyon's red soil, were neatly tended by surviving Lamb family members who lived in the area. Ed had even cleared a road through the brush for the Lambs so they wouldn't have to make their own way through the hostile, waist-high growth. The cemetery, hidden from the main road by bushes, served as a reminder that a century ago life and death were all done on the same land.

"I want to be cremated and have my ashes buried here, too," Ed said, walking around the cemetery that sat about a half mile from his home. "There's room for a few more in there."

Ed couldn't account for what he found outside the chain-link fence: four other graves, perhaps five—it was difficult to tell without taking a shovel in hand—sat askew to the fence, virtually hidden by the thick undergrowth. One was the grave of a dog; that much was certain from the drawing of a dog etched into a piece of pink flagstone that covered the ground. But the others had mounds of human dimension. Ed had no idea who or what was buried in them. There were no names on the stones, and all were decorated with faded plastic flowers. One even had an American flag.

"Are they other entities?" he asked me. "Who knows?"

*P*eople were serious about their ghosts and other difficult-to-explain phenomena. I soon understood why, particularly after I brought home the pottery shards that Archie Hanson gave me.

One night, I awoke from a deep sleep when I heard three loud knocks at my front door. By the third knock, I was upright in bed. At two in the morning, I had no intention of answering the door. I turned on a lamp and pulled the covers over my head. I didn't get to sleep until the first rays of the sun peeked into my bedroom.

About a week later, I woke up in the middle of a very still night to hear mournful and distant flute music. I thought perhaps I had left the radio on in my kitchen, but I wasn't about to get out of bed to check. I tried to sleep but couldn't. That morning, I checked the radio. I had turned it off the night before.

A few days later, I carefully broached the subject with an urban expatriate I felt I could trust. I told her the story. She listened quietly and then told me that other people who had taken shards and other items from ancient Anasazi sites also reported hearing knocks on their doors in the middle of the night. Others had heard flute music in the wee hours. Without telling these people I was conducting an informal survey, I asked them about this phenomenon. After a great deal of reluctance, most people shared their experiences. The similarities in their stories and mine were astounding. Yes, they had heard the knocks on the door in the middle of the night. Yes, they had heard the flute music. Some had heard both, and some of them admitted they had returned the shards to the sites where they had found them.

"People think you're crazy when you talk about this sort of thing, so we don't talk about it," said one woman who had heard knocks on her door and experienced other middle-of-the-night weirdness. Weeks after conducting my survey, I stood in my kitchen and looked at the pottery shards neatly laid out on the counter. Were my experiences the result of the power of suggestion? Had I subconsciously taken to heart the warnings about leaving shards where they were?

I didn't tell anyone else about my experiences, lest they think I was crazy. Many already thought I was a native New Yorker. The shards? I kept them.

Chapter 20

Final Days

The last weeks of school were relatively relaxed, though Harold still wasn't able to concentrate on his schoolwork. Stephen wasn't letting up. There were still six weeks left, and the teacher was bent on trying to shape a boy who still needed shaping.

"Focus," said Stephen, when he spotted the boy talking with Hoshi instead of reading an essay. Harold returned to his book, but within minutes he was talking again.

"You're playing," Stephen told the boy. "Find another place to sit."

Harold picked up his books and moved to an empty table, and only then did he make an effort to do his work. Minutes later, however, he and Hoshi pantomimed a conversation. Stephen couldn't see the two boys since he was administering a reading comprehension and vocabulary test to several students. When Harold finished his silent conversation with Hoshi, he began talking to another classmate, this time aloud. Stephen shot a stern look at the boy.

"Do not talk. She's taking a test, and you're studying for one," said Stephen, as he spotted Harold chatting with the sweet-tempered girl who was, indeed, trying to take a test. As Stephen admonished the boy, Hoshi began talking to another classmate. Sometimes keeping the school quiet was like putting out grass fires.

"Hoshi, concentrate," said Stephen. "Find another place to sit."

Hoshi found another chair, not far from Harold, but Hoshi didn't concentrate either. Stephen tried to wring the last bit of work from his students, but they weren't of a collective mind to write essays, do math, or read books. The final days ranked as the most difficult ones for Stephen, as they do for all teachers. Stephen kept the students focused while he ran on fumes himself from an overstuffed school calendar. He looked forward to the end of May, when his summer break began. But there were loose ends to tie up. Harold and Hoshi were two of them.

From his teacher's table, Stephen continued monitoring the two boys. They were quick to put their noses in their books when they sensed Stephen was about to look up from his table. On one occasion, the teacher was quicker than Harold. The boy had closed his book.

"I know you put your work away and you think you're done," Stephen said, rising from his chair. "Show me where you are in your book."

A panicked look crossed Harold's face. Just once, Stephen thought, it would be a great day if Harold did his work without the teacher having to relentlessly ride the boy. Harold opened the page in the grammar book he had been working from. Stephen was satisfied, perhaps even a bit surprised, at how many pages Harold had managed to read. When he concentrated, Harold was capable of doing quality work.

After the midmorning recess was over, Harold and Hoshi returned to their seats and began chatting once more, this time about the new Play Station magazine that Harold had brought to school. As Hoshi looked at the magazine advertising the latest computer games, Harold began playing with a classmate's note-book, sliding it toward another classmate. The notebook fell on the floor several times, its cover getting torn and dirty on each fall. Finally, the classmate sitting next to Harold picked it up and took the notebook to its owner, a second-grade girl who was sit-ting at another table.

The girl looked at her frayed notebook and looked at the table where Harold sat. A classmate sitting next to Harold quietly pointed at the boy as the guilty party. Harold was surprised when the girl walked up behind him and hit him on the head three times with her notebook. Harold winced.

"Leave my notebook alone!" she huffed, returning to her desk.

"Ouch!" Harold exclaimed. "Why did you do that?"

Harold rose from his chair and indignantly walked to Stephen. The moment was a rare opportunity for Harold to turn in one of his classmates, as they had done to him on more occasions than Stephen could count.

The girl watched Harold from her chair, as he re-created the surprise attack for Stephen. The teacher stole looks at the third grader. Then, without being summoned, she went to the teacher's table to plead her case. She did so with less drama. Stephen talked to the girl in hushed tones as she looked at the floor. Before she returned to her table, she stopped at Harold's chair.

"I'm sorry," she huffed.

As she walked away, she turned her head and stuck out her tongue at Harold. Stephen shot a weary look in the direction of the two students.

For Harold, who had been tormented by classmates all year long, even a small victory was a sweet one. For most of the lunch hour, he replayed for his classmates every detail of his triumph.

*G*raduation day unfolded with all the beauty of a late spring day in McElmo Canyon. Stephen and Teresa had spent the previous weeks designing certificates on their computers. The citations went to students who completed the year on the *A* and *B* honor roll. Other children received awards for reading twenty or more books. Perfect attendance was also rewarded. Every child received a $5 gift certificate to a Cortez bookstore.

The teacher and his aide had grown close during the long hours they had spent planning the school's numerous field trips and programs. They had worked together on the school's Christmas program and Battle Rock's float in the Christmas parade. They had planned the numerous walking tours of the canyon. Now, they teamed up one final time to organize the awards ceremony. The children's accomplishments masked what had been a gritty year for the teacher.

At home, with Susan, he had quietly pondered his future at the school. More than once, they had discussed his leaving Battle Rock. After seven years at the school, Stephen was weary of the acrimony and the demands. The discord with Kim Lindgren had subsided in the final weeks of the school year, but Stephen instinctively knew there would be more conflict. He felt the two had unfinished business.

Stephen pushed all the unpleasantness away on the final day of school. With only minutes to spare, he and Teresa finished preparations for the awards ceremony. The teacher opened the school door to students and parents beginning to gather on the Sticker Patch. Children sat on the floor in front of the long blackboard, while nearly twenty parents took the chairs or stood at the back of the room.

Every child received hearty applause from the assembled parents and grandparents. Battle Rock was an extension of the home, and if each child had twenty-five brothers and sisters, each parent had multiple children. Parents unable to attend because of jobs didn't have to worry about their children. Those students received ovations as robust as classmates whose parents were in attendance. Some parents had their issues with Stephen, but virtually nothing got in the way of supporting the children.

When the last of the awards were parceled out to the children, Stephen presented Teresa with an accolade that caught her by surprise. She had labored all year to produce the *Battle Rock Bulletin,* a chatty newsletter that included birthdays, school projects, and field trips. Anyone who wanted to get a sense of the school only needed to read the monthly newsletter. She had also headed the school's Accountability Committee, Battle Rock's version of the Parent Teacher Association.

She laughed nervously as she walked to the front of the school to accept the certificate.

"I want to thank my agent," she said joking.

When the ceremony was over, Stephen ushered the crowd outside so that he and Teresa could set up the room for cake and pink lemonade. When everything was set and Stephen appeared at the door, he noticed the children had pushed the parents to the back of the line. In his teacher's voice, Stephen ordered the students to step aside and let the parents pass. The children parted like the Red Sea, and parents, aunts and uncles, grandparents, cousins, brothers and sisters climbed the stairs and stood in line for cake.

Then came the moment the children had eagerly awaited: the school's traditional end-of-the-year water fight. No one was off-limits. Not Stephen, parents, nor the other guests.

"Will you be my ally?" Harold asked a classmate, as they filled multicolored balloons with water. Before long, Stephen emerged from the school in shorts, a white T-shirt, and tennis shoes. He opened his arms in a sacrificial stance for the children. Armed with a large water pistol, tiny Tim Jeter was one of the first to squirt the teacher. The children laughed and shrieked as they attacked Stephen.

He was soaked in five minutes, as the Sticker Patch quickly became a chaotic scene of children attacking classmates with water guns and water balloons. Then parents joined in as the balloons were flung through the air, dropping on the parents sitting on the picnic tables. Friendly fire, one parent called it, as he ducked into the school's cloakroom. I followed him and watched the melee from the safety of the cloakroom.

Two students gathered trash cans from the school and went to the ditch and came back to the playground carrying the medium-sized trash cans. They began dumping the water on classmates. The water was foul; it was treated sewage from the good people of Cortez.

"There's a reason the water is brown," said Kim Lindgren to other parents. The parents laughed, but they increasingly crowded the door of the school as water balloons hoisted into the air fell nearer the school's steps.

In forty-five minutes the water fight was over. The Sticker Patch was drenched, and one by one parents and their children went home. Stephen went inside to change into dry clothes. By lunchtime the school and the playground were empty. Only the janitor was present, a lonely figure as he swept the steps to the one-room school. Stephen lingered for an hour, putting away papers, giving the room a once over, and then he turned off his computer. He bounded down the steps and drove out of the school's gravel parking lot, and his white Ford Explorer disappeared around a bend in the road. He had survived another school year, and that was no easy task in a place like McElmo Canyon.

Afterword

Stephen Hanson spent six weeks that summer at Oxford University, where he continued working on a master's degree through Middlebury College's program for rural teachers. But the refreshment of a summer abroad quickly faded when he returned and began confronting issues at Battle Rock. In the wake of Kim's complaints, Stephen decided to restructure the school. His campaign produced results altogether unexpected.

He assumed more teaching responsibilities and assigned to his aide, Teresa, most of the school's administrative duties. But he sowed trouble for himself when he changed the job descriptions of the two part-time teachers who taught kindergarten and math and science. The math and science teacher resigned. Then the kindergarten teacher quit the day before school began. Stephen quickly replaced the two teachers with one, a young woman who had recently graduated from Fort Lewis College in nearby Durango.

One crisis was averted, but another loomed when the rancor flared again between Stephen and Kim. Now with a new teacher in place, Stephen startled everyone when he resigned in early October, just a month into the new school year.

"Doing my work at Battle Rock Charter School has never been easy," he wrote in his five-paragraph resignation letter. Without mentioning Kim by name, he wrote, "In this age of expanding information we could never be all things to all people. Indeed, some parents in the past have recognized that Battle Rock School was not working for them and have been able to make a decision to withdraw their children." They had done so, he noted, without casting negative aspersions on Battle Rock's teachers, board members, and other parents.

As happens in a small community, word of Stephen's imminent departure traveled quickly. When the school board met two weeks later to accept Stephen's resignation and hire a replacement, the teacher arrived at the school and was stunned to find Battle Rock crowded with parents. Some parents thanked him for his years at the school. But many more asked him to stay. Some even cried as they asked him to reconsider his decision. There were a lot of moist eyes in the school that night.

Kim also attended the meeting. "Stephen, I never meant to hurt you, and I never meant for you to quit." She then proceeded to tell the teacher and those assembled that Battle Rock could do better by its students.

"What makes you think this isn't a great school, miss?" asked one parent with four children enrolled.

The meeting that autumn night consumed hours, the lights spilling out of the school's narrow windows as the shadows lengthened across McElmo Canyon. At the conclusion of the meeting, Stephen reconsidered his resignation. He told the school board and the assembled parents that he would stay through the school year. But the emotional gathering that night was only half of the drama. Behind closed doors earlier that evening, the Battle Rock board had removed Kim as its vice president.

"We, the duly elected officers and members of the Battle Rock Charter School Governing Board of Directors," the document read, "do hereby petition for the removal of Board member Kim

Lindgren." The petition said Kim's actions were "detrimental to the school, and do not respect the mission, philosophy, or goals of Battle Rock Charter School."

Kim's ouster was more than a show of support for Stephen. In the weeks following Stephen's resignation, some parents had quietly told board members that they would leave Battle Rock if Stephen left the school. Board members didn't want a repeat of the Botticelli mess. There would be no second mass exodus from the school. Not this time.

I had watched the conflict unfold in the year I attended Battle Rock and knew the discord was taking a toll on the teacher. I was nonetheless astonished when I read the news about Stephen's resignation via a short email from Susan, his wife. Two weeks later, I learned about the tumultuous school board meeting when I woke up one morning and, over coffee, checked my email. I had received several long missives from parents and interested observers who replayed the long board meeting, Kim's ouster, and Stephen's about-face. After a year of listening to locals tell the same stories with materially different facts, I was struck by the consistency of the accounts I received that morning. I also received an unmarked envelope a few days later in the mail that contained Stephen's resignation letter and copies of Battle Rock board minutes, which contained Kim's complaints about the school and its deficiencies. About six months later I returned to Cortez, in March 2001, to find out what had happened.

"This was less about me and more about people upset about an outsider coming in and trying to change their school," Stephen quietly told me in his home one evening. No one knew better than he how locals turned quickly on someone who threatened the school with change. Stephen had survived another challenge, but Kim wasn't so fortunate.

"It was ugly," she said in her McElmo Canyon home. "After the meeting, one parent came up to me and said, 'This school needs a scapegoat, and this year, you're it.'" No one who knew Battle Rock's history disagreed with that assessment.

Kim found herself ostracized wherever she went, whether it was the grocery store or other errands in Cortez. "Whenever I see people, they can't look me in the eye," she said. But she maintained her dignity, greeting people nonetheless. Following her removal, she elected to home school her daughters two days a week, sending the girls to Battle Rock for the rest of the week. But her convictions about the school were firm. She likened its shortcomings to a ladder missing several steps. Kim drew consolation, however small, from Stephen's revamping the school to reflect many of her suggestions.

Stephen continued teaching for the remainder of the school year, but at a school board meeting I attended during my return visit, he announced his seventh year would be his last. The unanimous vote by the board to accept Stephen's resignation was anticlimactic. There was no discussion of the recent events, nor were there any references to Stephen's long and difficult tenure at the school. What was there left to say?

"It's time to leave," he told the board firmly.

But Stephen had built himself a bridge. He was named director of the Colorado Rural Charter School Network, the association of six rural schools that he helped create. Because of his own issues with Battle Rock's school boards, Stephen was intent on using some of the network's money to train new school board members. "All the schools have gotten into trouble with their boards," he said.

The conflicts that defined much of Stephen's life at Battle Rock begged larger questions. Could the nation's surviving one-room schools endure the sometimes destructive mix of urban and rural values? Were these schools even practicable options in a new century? Battle Rock was protected by the simple fact that it provided an educational option for parents and children in a community where there were precious few. Nontraditional public schools like Battle Rock—and other rural charter schools, and even urban charters that embraced academic themes of every kind—were seen as cornerstones in efforts to improve public education. No school movement embodied that notion more fully than the charter school movement's break-the-mold mentality. Though many locals complained about the expense of maintaining Battle Rock, the school was actually cheaper to operate than a traditional public school. Battle Rock received 80 percent of the funding a traditional public school received in Colorado. If there were financial questions about Battle Rock's future or those of its sister schools in the Colorado Rural Charter School Network, the Colorado legislature settled them by increasing to 95 percent the amount of public funding a charter school received in the 2000–2001 school year. The school generated the remaining 5 percent of its budget with fund-raisers and foundation dollars.

But in a new century, one-room schools and their communities continued to face considerable pressures. Most of it came from central school administrations in the name of economy. After modest year-to-year increases through the mid-1990s, the number of one-room schools began declining again at the end of the twentieth century. By 2000, there were 423 one-room, or "one-teacher," schools, as compared with 476 three years earlier, according to the U.S. Department of Education. Consolidation was the reason most often given for the closings.

Even as the number of one-room schools declined, so did the urban migration to rural America. After a torrid pace in the first half of the 1990s, the great march out of the cities to rural communities slowed in the decade's second half, according to the U.S. Department of Agriculture. The USDA also noted that urban people continued to move to rural communities in the new century, albeit in smaller numbers. The rural economy also lost some steam, reflecting the overall malaise of the American economy. But even with the contractions, many rural communities were in the best shape they had been in decades.

*E*ven with all the challenges I faced, I found myself enamored with the place. I'm not sure when I realized Montezuma County had become my adopted hometown, or that my rented farm-house with uneven floors off the gravel lane had become my home. But at some point during the winter, I surprised myself one night while sitting in my living room on a lumpy secondhand recliner. Maybe, I thought, I could find a way to permanently stay. I hadn't experienced a sense of community this strong in two decades, at least, and the feeling was intoxicating.

Maybe I realized the place was special during the Reverend Don Henderson's sermons about forgiveness and faith at the First Assembly of God Church. Or in the quite moments I enjoyed in my old farmhouse, or during my walks in the pasture that sat behind my house. Or in dining on simple meals in the homes of families who had raised the food themselves. Those dinners of home-raised chicken or beef, squash and potatoes, lettuce and toma-toes, and homemade bread topped by homemade jams and jellies of grapes and plums and peaches were every bit as rich as the meals I had enjoyed in some of Manhattan's finer restaurants.

By spring I found myself seriously considering staying on in Cortez and nearly applied for the vacant managing editor's job at the *Cortez Journal.* But after three months of soul-searching, I decided that cities still offered more positives than negatives, and I left Montezuma County in the summer of 2000 for Los Angeles and a new teaching job at the University of Southern California. I left my rural home reluctantly, but I left a fundamentally differ-ent person.

Living quietly and simply had helped restore balance to a life sorely out of kilter, as it had for Bill and Teresa Blakney and oth-ers who found a second breath in a rural setting. For most of my adult life, I had worked and done nothing else, and the imbalance finally surfaced in Cortez, where I was forced to face hard truths about myself. I lost nearly thirty pounds because of all the walk-ing and hiking I did and the better diet I put on my table. I didn't watch television for a year. I didn't miss it. I read more books in that year than in any other I remember. And my quality of life was better than it had been in Boulder, where I had lived, and a huge improvement from my life in New York City, so rushed and overstuffed with material possessions and values that ultimately became clutter, or did not work, in a place like Cortez.

The virtues of small-town life that Teresa had enthused about in the fall and that I had pondered again in the spring during conversations with Rev. Henderson had reshaped me. On a warm August morning, as I drove out of town for Los Angeles, I took in the full majesty of the Sleeping Ute Mountain and promised myself not to forget the lessons I had learned.

Selected Bibliography

This book is based on more than two hundred interviews with private and public citizens of Montezuma County, Cortez, and McElmo Canyon, Colorado, over the course of a year, from August 1999 through August 2000, and in March 2001. For background on charter schools, corporal punishment, the national education reform movement, and school finance, I relied on the dozens of articles I wrote on these topics from 1990 to 1995 as a national education correspondent for the *New York Times*.

On rural population trends

Johnson, Kenneth M., and Calvin L. Beale. "The Rural Rebound." *The Wilson Quarterly* (spring 1998). (Johnson, of Loyola University in Chicago, and Beale, of the U.S. Department of Agriculture, use the U.S. Census Bureau's definition of *rural*: "non-metropolitan" counties without urban centers of 50,000 or more.)

Lapping, Mark B., Thomas L. Daniels, and John W. Keller. *Rural Planning and Development in the United States*. New York: Guilford Press, 1989.

U.S. Department of Agriculture. *Rural Conditions and Trends* 9, no. 2 (February 1999).

———. *Rural Conditions and Trends* 11, no. 2 (December 2000).

On rural schools and their teachers

Gulliford, Andrew. *America's Country Schools.* 3rd ed. Boulder: University Press of Colorado, 1996.

Harmon, Hobart. "Rural Schools in a Global Economy." *School Board News,* March 25, 1997.

"Lessons of a Century." *Education Week,* September 15, 1999.

Rural Challenge Research and Evaluation Program. *Living and Learning in Rural Schools and Communities: Lessons From the Field.* Report to the Annenberg Rural Challenge. Cambridge, Mass.: Harvard University Graduate School of Education, February 1999.

Rural School and Community Trust. Annual Report 2001. Washington, D.C.

On the rural economy

Center for the New West. *Strong Growth Drives a Dramatic Economic Transition in the West.* Denver, 1996.

Montezuma County Economic Development Board. *Montezuma County Economic Trends, Components and Issues.* Cortez, Colo., April 18, 2000.

National Agricultural Statistics Service, U.S. Department of Agriculture. *Agricultural Land Values: Average Farm Real Estate Values Continue Upward.* Washington, D.C.: March 2000.

"Southwest Colorado Jobless Rates Top State Charts." *Cortez Journal,* February 8, 2000.

U.S. Department of Agriculture. *Rural Conditions and Trends* 9, no. 2 (February 1999).

Various state of Colorado employment and economic index reports.

On rural crime and gun control

"Agency: Gun Deaths Decline in 1990s." Associated Press. April 7, 2001. (A report on the study by the Centers for Disease Control and Prevention on gun deaths.)

Federal Bureau of Investigation, U.S. Department of Justice. *Crime in the United States.* Washington, D.C., 1998.

"Guns in America." (A four-part series on gun control issues that appeared throughout 1997 in Hearst newspapers.)

"Methodist Churches Offer Cable Gun Locks to Everyone." *Cortez Journal,* October 5, 1999.

"Targeting the Real Problem." *Cortez Journal,* January 6, 2000. (Opinion piece about local and regional gun attitudes.)

Index

PublicAffairs is a publishing house founded in 1997. It is a tribute to the standards, values, and flair of three persons who have served as mentors to countless reporters, writers, editors, and book people of all kinds, including me.

I. F. Stone, proprietor of *I. F. Stone's Weekly*, combined a commitment to the First Amendment with entrepreneurial zeal and reporting skill and became one of the great independent journalists in American history. At the age of eighty, Izzy published *The Trial of Socrates*, which was a national bestseller. He wrote the book after he taught himself ancient Greek.

Benjamin C. Bradlee was for nearly thirty years the charismatic editorial leader of *The Washington Post*. It was Ben who gave the *Post* the range and courage to pursue such historic issues as Watergate. He supported his reporters with a tenacity that made them fearless, and it is no accident that so many became authors of influential, best-selling books.

Robert L. Bernstein, the chief executive of Random House for more than a quarter century, guided one of the nation's premier publishing houses. Bob was personally responsible for many books of political dissent and argument that challenged tyranny around the globe. He is also the founder and was the longtime chair of Human Rights Watch, one of the most respected human rights organizations in the world.

      .   .   .

For fifty years, the banner of Public Affairs Press was carried by its owner, Morris B. Schnapper, who published Gandhi, Nasser, Toynbee, Truman, and about 1,500 other authors. In 1983 Schnapper was described by *The Washington Post* as "a redoubtable gadfly." His legacy will endure in the books to come.

Peter Osnos, *Publisher*